INTELLECTUAL
CAPITAL

INTELLECTUAL CAPITAL

REALIZING YOUR COMPANY'S TRUE VALUE BY FINDING ITS HIDDEN ROOTS

Leif Edvinsson
and Michael S. Malone

HarperBusiness
A Division of HarperCollins*Publishers*

HarperCollins books may be purchased for educational, business, or sales promotional use. For information please write: Special Markets Department, HarperCollins Publishers, Inc., 10 East 53rd Street, New York, NY 10022.

FIRST EDITION

Designed by Irving Perkins Associates

Library of Congress Cataloging-in-Publication Data

Edvinsson, Leif.
Intellectual capital : realizing your company's true value by finding
its hidden roots / by Leif Edvinsson and Michael S. Malone.
p.   cm.
Includes index.
ISBN 0-88730-841-4
1. Creative ability in business.   2. Human capital.   I. Malone,
Michael S. (Michael Shawn), 1954–   .   II. Title.
HD53.E34   1997
658.4′09—dc21   96-51533

97 98 99 00 01 ❖/RRD 10 9 8 7 6 5 4 3 2 1

To the future of my daughters Marie, and Sophie,
and the next generations
—L. E.

To Tad and Skipper, that the world
may better value their talents
—M. S. M.

Contents

Foreword

At the beginning of 1997 an American consortium, only fifteen years old, soared to the top of the world's stock-market-value league. Can you name the consortium? Hint: By the start of 1997, global investors had bid it up to $220 billion, far past such perennial champions as General Electric ($170 billion) and Nippon Telegraph and Telephone ($94 billion).

The answer is Wintel.

Wintel? Okay, it's a trick. Wintel is not a real consortium, although for all intents it operates like one. It is actually an amalgam. It is derived from Microsoft's Windows operating systems software and Intel, the chip colossus. All wordplay aside, Microsoft is worth $100 billion—of which Bill Gates owns 24 percent—and Intel, $120 billion.

Think about these figures for a while. They are stunning, and the brain does not wrap around them too easily.

Intellectual capital, of course, has always been a decisive factor in the rise of civilizations, organizations, and people. For at least 60,000 years our ancestors, the Cro-Magnons, lived side by side with the Neanderthals. Then, about 30,000 years ago, the Neanderthals disappeared.

Why did one species survive and the other perish? Both used tools and language, but the Cro-Magnons had a lunar calendar. Soon they correlated the passing days with the migratory patterns of bison, elk, and red deer. This insight was dutifully recorded on cave-wall paintings and in sets of 28 notches on reindeer antlers.

Hungry for meat, the Cro-Magnon was taught that all he had to do was wait at a river crossing on certain days, spear in hand. In the meantime, the Neanderthals appear to have unwisely scattered their men and their scarce resources in search of random encounters. They allocated their resources poorly. They perished.

Intellectual capital made the difference. It always has. So why must you read Leif Edvinsson and Mike Malone's *Intellectual Capital* now?

Three reasons. First is the Wintel story and others like it. Wealth creation is now a mental event. Microsoft's stock trades at ten times book value, which means that 90 percent of its value is intangible. It is software code, brand name, and marketing clout—all three of which come straight from the brains of people. No one know this better than Gates himself. In January 1997 he revealed to *Time* magazine the secret of Microsoft's Midas touch: "We win because we hire the smartest people. We improve products based on feedback, until they're the best. We have retreats each year where we think about where the world is heading." In other words, Gates continually works to increase Microsoft's intellectual capital.

Second, the information revolution—that one-two punch of computers and global networks—is exerting the same force on every company, and every industry, in the world: a radical reduction in the cost and time of obtaining information about your suppliers and markets. Given that ecology, it suddenly makes little sense to organize your company in a vertically integrated way. All around the world, companies and industries are "deverticalizing," as the old advantages of muscle and scale give way to smarts, connectivity, and speed. Today, your strategy is to figure out which horizontal layers in the supply chain are best for you.

But here is the catch: The choicest layers are reserved for those who best identify, nurture, and deploy their intellectual capital. Microsoft lives a more enviable life than do Texas PC makers, who have it better than Korean memory-chip factories, who live larger than Malaysian board stuffers . . . and so on down the value layers. Unless you understand your intellectual capital strengths and weaknesses, you cannot know where your company best belongs.

Third, because *Intellectual Capital* is a cracking good read, even as it informs. How many business books can you say that about?

Not that I agree with everything Edvinsson and Malone say. I'm skeptical, for instance, of a few particulars in their intellectual balance sheet. Some of the measurements, to me, smack of political correctness. But that's part of the debate to come, set in motion by the contents of this book. Edvinsson and Malone are the first to take a stand on intellectual capital measurement—and in the process created a book that is well researched, well intended, and sharply written.

Intellectual capital is about to be one of the hottest topics in business, and many books and articles on the subject are in the works. They'll have a hard time besting this one.

Rich Karlgaard
editor, *Forbes ASAP*
January 1997

INTELLECTUAL CAPITAL

The Hidden Roots of Value

Read a useful prospectus lately? How about an informative annual report?

How come few of these traditional reports anymore offer a clue about which emerging young company is about to take over the world, or about which established, blue-chip company is about to fall into a competitive black hole?

And even when these reports do manage to capture a glimmer of reality, how come those clues lie between the lines of the accompanying, barely legible text and not in bold type on the balance sheet? And why do brokerage houses publish buy or sell recommendations on stocks that seem to have nothing to do with the financial performance of the companies those stocks represent?

Most curious of all, why has the stock market set new records throughout the 1990s when the economy, even during upswings, is consistently weak?

The answer is that the traditional model of "accounting," which so beautifully described the operations of companies for a half millennium, is now failing to keep up with the revolution taking place in business. Like the organization chart, printed corporate brochure, and employee handbook, corporate financial documents are increasingly proving themselves too static and hidebound to keep up with the modern organization, with its fluid structure, strategic partnering, empowered employees,

1

groupware, multimedia network marketing, and vital reservoirs of human intellectual resources.

The chilling fact is this: At this moment we have no idea which companies, large or small, young or old, have sustainable organizational capability.

Rich Karlgaard, editor of *Forbes ASAP*, identified this disaster and what it would take to fix it in a 1993 editorial:

> As an index, book value is dead as a doornail, an artifact of the Industrial Age. We live in the Information Age, of course, though remarkably few people have come to terms with that fact. Failure to understand the declining relevance of book value—and the hard assets that form the ratio's numerator—is proof of this.
>
> Human intelligence and intellectual resources are now any company's most valuable assets.
>
> The economist who comes up with a better measure of core value will have to account for the new intangible assets so ascendant today. . . . [For now] society utterly lacks the metrics needed to measure this new source of wealth.[1]

There have always been occasional and temporary gaps between market perception and accounting reality. But now that gap is turning into a chasm. And that in turn suggests we are looking not at a temporary aberration but at a systemic flaw in the way we measure value. A fundamental discrepancy between the story told on corporate balance sheets and the real one played out daily by the organizations themselves.

The business pages of America's newspapers are filled with examples. Southwest Airlines is valued greater than veteran airlines many times its size. Intel suffers a major scandal from flaws in its flagship Pentium chip and its stock price barely breaks stride. Netscape, a $17 million company with fifty employees, goes public with an initial stock offering that values the company at $3 billion by the end of the day. Microsoft, an $8 billion company, announced its Windows 95 operating system and sees its stock climb to more than $100 per share, making the company more valuable than Chrysler or Boeing.

It has become obvious that the real value of these companies cannot be determined by only traditional accounting measures. The worth of an Intel or Microsoft lies *not* in bricks and mortar, or even in inventories, but in another, intangible kind of asset: **Intellectual Capital.**

In the words of Walter Wriston in his influential book *The Twilight of Sovereignty,* "Indeed, the new source of wealth is not material, it is information, knowledge applied to work to create value."[2]

TOWARD A DEFINITION

What is Intellectual Capital? Until now, the definition has been elusive. But in recent years, driven by necessity, individuals and groups in diverse disciplines have begun to tackle the challenge of finding a standardized explanation.

SEC commissioner Steven M. H. Wallman includes under his definition of Intellectual Capital not just human brainpower but also brand names and trademarks, even assets booked at historic costs that have transformed through time into something of greater value (like a forest bought a century ago that now is prime real estate). All, in his words, are "assets currently valued at zero on the balance sheet."[3]

Other researchers include in their definition of Intellectual Capital such factors as technology leadership, ongoing employee training, even speed of response to client service calls.

For venture capitalist and business writer William Davidow (*The Virtual Corporation*), "There's a need to move to a new level in accounting," he says, "one that measures a company's *momentum* in terms of market position, customer loyalty, quality, etc. By not valuing these dynamic perspectives, we are misstating the value of a company as badly as if we were making mistakes in addition."[4]

3

For H. Thomas Johnson, professor of business administration at Portland (Oregon) State University, Intellectual Capital hides within that most mysterious traditional accounting entry, "goodwill." The difference, he says, is that traditionally goodwill emphasized unusual, but real, assets such as trademarks. By comparison, he says, Intellectual Capital looks beyond to more ineffable assets such as the ability of a company to learn and adapt.[5]

Wrote *Industry Week* in early 1996:

> Managers struggl[e] in the here and now to adjust to the shift in the center of economic gravity from the management and measurement of physical and financial assets to the cultivation and leverage of knowledge as the most significant acts of value creation.
>
> And it applies as much to Microsoft as it does to a knitting mill in the wilds of Canada weaving berets on a machine bought by the proprietor's great-grandfather in 1919. Ask an executive from either firm what percentage of total value they would attribute to intangible assets—everything from individual skills and know-how to IT systems, designs, and trademarks to supplier relationships and customer franchise—and you get the same answer: upward of 80 percent.
>
> Then ask them to contemplate the ratio of value siphoned off into the accounting hot-air balloon called "goodwill" over assets actually inked into the balance sheet and you get paroxysms.[6]

The magazine goes on to quote an angry Lars Kolind, president of Danish hearing-aid maker Oticon Holding A/S, whose firm has grown in market value from 150 million Danish kroner in 1991 to 2.4 billion today—yet only 400 million of those kroner show on the balance sheet. Says Kolind, "All of our accounting, all of the rules of the government and stock exchange, all the resources, everything is focused on the equity, which is absolutely stupid because the 2 billion Danish Kroner of intellectual capital is five times as high!"[7]

Some observers have even suggested that intellectual capital actually subsumes what we usually think of as fixed assets, which on closer inspection prove to be less fixed than we thought. For example, Gary Hamel, a professor at the London School of Business, has argued that an asset is really only a perception of an opportunity about which a majority of people have agreed.[8]

Whatever definition is used, it is apparent that the value of Intellectual Capital in the world's businesses is immense. Charles Handy, also of the London School of Business, has estimated that these intellectual assets may typically be worth three or four times a company's tangible book value.[9] According to Morgan Stanley's World Index, the average value of companies on the world's stock exchanges is two times book value. In the United States, corporate market value typically ranges from two to nine times book value.[10]

Says Professor Keith Bradley of the Open Business School (U.K.):

> Over the past twenty years there has been a significant widening of the gap between the values of enterprises state in corporate balance sheets and investors assessment of those values. [The median market-to-book value ratio for U.S. public corporations over a twenty-year period between 1973 and 1993 increased from 0.82 to 1.692.] The gap in 1992 indicates that roughly forty percent of market value of the median U.S. public corporation was missing from the balance sheet. For knowledge-intensive corporations, the percentage assets missing from the balance sheet is over one hundred.
>
> These distortions are also reflected in recent U.S. acquisitions. An examination of the relationship between the price paid for U.S. acquisitions over a thirteen-year period between 1981 and 1993 of some 391 transactions with a median value of $1.9 billion shows that the mean of the price of acquisition-to-book value is 4.4. This indicates that, on average, the real values of the acquired corporations were about four and a half times larger than the values reported in the balance sheets. Acquisitions of knowledge-intense companies had price-to-book values larger than ten. . . .

Do we have the tools to manage these hidden assets? The simple answer is "no, we don't."[11]

The Microsofts and Netscapes of the world support Handy's and Bradley's extraordinary estimates; they show that even without a common yardstick for measuring Intellectual Capital, the recognition of its presence by informed observers will establish a value for a firm that dwarfs its balance sheet.

In the words of Judy Lewent, chief financial officer of Merck & Co., "In a knowledge-based company, the accounting system doesn't capture anything really."[12] To which one can only add: At the dawn of the twenty-first century, which companies *aren't* knowledge based?

Certainly the companies themselves know the hard reality: A survey by the Institute of Management Accounting found that 64 percent of corporate controllers in the United States said their companies were actively experimenting with new ways of measuring performance.[13] When nearly two-thirds of the companies in the world's largest economy have accepted the need for change, we no longer have an interesting new trend, but a revolution.

The accounting industry knows too. In 1991, the American Institute of Certified Public Accountants (AICPA) formed a Special Committee on Financial Reporting to address a growing concern about the relevance of orthodox financial reporting and disclosure to the modern economy. Three years later the committee issued its report. It found a number of substantial areas for improvement—improvements that, in the words of Sarah Mavrinac and Terry Boyle of Ernst & Young, Boston,

could be realized with 1) the provision of information about corporate plans, opportunities, risks, and uncertainties, 2) better alignment of external reporting systems with internal management control and information systems, and, 3) enhanced discussion of the non-financial performance factors that create longer-term value. Underlying these recommendations is the assumption that non-financial performance data have value relevance and can be effectively used by investors as *leading indicators of future financial performance.*"[14]

Mavrinac and Boyle went on to conduct their own study—and come to the same conclusion: "Analysts *do* treat non-financial performance data as leading indicators of future financial performance"[15] as well as, to a lesser degree, share purchase recommendations and short-term earnings forecasts.

PLAYING THE MIDDLE

Some people have grown very wealthy off this gap between perceived value and accounting value. "We've essentially created an inefficient market where speculators can take advantage of the resulting volatility," says Davidow.[16]

A few major industry players are frank enough to admit this advantage. Robert G. Herwick, president of Herwick Capital Management, is particularly forthright about this inequity: "My ability to make informed projections is my competitive advantage."[17]

The big brokerage houses, with their teams of analysts, can track the top talents as they move through industry, or develop databases on a company's patents and other intellectual property holdings. With access to the company, they can sometimes identify a hot newcomer or spot a deep, but hidden, flaw in a current high flyer.

But this lack of common practices for disclosing and visualizing Intellectual Capital hurts all stakeholders and investors. They, too, can miss a subtle change in tenor or the loss of a key knowledge-carrying employee that signals the coming eclipse of a corporate star. And more often, they simply don't spot until the last minute the private new start-up that is about to change the world.

As a result, too many deserving companies are underoptimized and undercapitalized, and thus sometimes are unable to complete their destiny. Meanwhile, other, troubled firms are artificially propped up until they collapse, pulling down shareholders and investors with them.

And that is just the problem among professional economists, investors, and the companies they watch. For the tens of millions of small private investors, armed with only a prospectus or annual report and the pages of the daily newspaper, the current system is patently unfair. How can the small investor ever possibly obtain the nuanced, dynamic information he or she needs? Certainly that shareholder can't get it from the financial tables in the annual report.

And almost forgotten in this disaster are the larger, hidden social costs of this dislocation: unemployment, reduced productivity, and diminished national competitiveness. An economy that cannot properly measure its value cannot accurately distribute its resources nor properly reward its citizens.

One organization that has investigated this potential disaster is the Competitiveness Policy Council. Its Capital Allocation Subcouncil looked into the failure of traditional accounting to value indirect, "soft" assets and reported that

> anachronistic rules suppress the overall level of business investment, and investment in long-term and intangible business assets, such as R&D and work force training, in particular . . . by restricting the amount of capital available per worker and capital in a way that undermines growth in worker productivity and company revenues. Such growth is the key to sustainable increases in wages and standards.[18]

In an age when not only companies but entire product categories can disappear overnight, and where competitors may change their relationships and their relative market shares daily, earnings statements and balance sheets offer little more than snapshots of where the company has *been*. Even worse, most of those snapshots are skewed or aimed at the wrong subject. After all, who cares how much land the company owns if its technology is not going to be accepted by the market? And how valuable is inventory, except as landfill, if the market has adopted a different standard?

By the same token, the balance sheet offers no hint of a company's memories, traditions, and philosophy. It doesn't tell how much they are worth or set off alarms when, through management decisions or employee layoffs, they are lost. The result is often a kind of corporate Alzheimer's, whereby a company busy watching the bottom line loses its institutional memory, and thus itself, without ever noticing the loss.

This confusion reigns not only at the corporate and equity levels. Rather, the confused signals found there suggest that the whole economy may be distorted and operating well below its capacity. Much of the U.S. election debate of 1992 was about the state of the economy. After a market crash and years of dismaying books and articles about how America had lost its competitive edge to Japan and its economic leadership to western Europe, most citizens were convinced the American Century was over and the only hope for the future was to cut the losses and defend the economic borders. Meanwhile, Japan and Europe became complacent, the former about its industrial prowess, the latter by its social model.

The last four years have taught us that almost everything we thought we knew was wrong. Beneath the depressed economic surface of giant old companies suffering losses and layoffs, a business revolution was taking place that never appeared in the statistics. New kinds of companies were being created that were more flexible, more adaptive, and more fluid in their structures, producing "smart" products and services that featured mass customization, customer participation in product design and manufacture, and the linking of suppliers, distributors, and strategic partners into chains of common destiny. It is these knowledge-intensive firms, found in almost every industry from semiconductors to steel mills, that have led the revolution, leaving other companies—and other nations—to catch up.[19]

These agile, "virtual," or "imaginary"[20] corporations, as they have been called, feature at their philosophical center an entirely different notion of what constitutes an asset. In a world where R&D, manufacturing, and sales may be performed by a partner in a strategic alliance or even a customer, such traditional balance sheet line items as plant, equipment, and land no longer offer much insight into a company's current competitiveness or future earnings potential. And how, for example, does one compute the value of knowledge delivered? Even inventory becomes essentially meaningless when the very notion of a product model begins to disappear into the new reality of a customized product for every customer produced on demand.

Except when the government demands they report the old-fashioned way, what really matters to these companies (and smart investors) is the Intellectual Capital that keeps a company attractive and sustainable in its value creation.

THE ROOTS OF VALUE

Perhaps the best way to appreciate the role of Intellectual Capital is metaphorical. If we picture a company as a living organism, say a tree, then what is described in organization charts, annual reports, quarterly statements, company brochures, and other documents is the trunk, branches, and leaves. The smart investor scrutinizes this tree in search of ripe fruit to harvest.

But to assume that this is the entire tree because it represents everything immediately visible is obviously a mistake. Half the mass or more of that tree is underground in the root system. And whereas the flavor of the fruit and the color of the leaves provides evidence of how healthy that tree is right now, understanding what is going on in the roots is a far more effective way to learn how healthy that tree will be in the years to come. The rot or parasite just now appearing thirty feet underground may well kill that tree that today looks in the prime of health.

That is what makes Intellectual Capital—the study of the roots of a company's value, the measurement of the hidden dynamic factors that underlie the visible company of buildings and products—so valuable.

What are these factors? According to research conducted by the Swedish insurance and financial services company Skandia, these factors typically take two forms:

1. *Human capital*. The combined knowledge, skill, innovativeness, and ability of the company's individual employees to meet the task at hand. It also includes the company's values, culture, and philosophy. Human capital cannot be owned by the company.

2. *Structural capital*. The hardware, software, databases, organizational structure, patents, trademarks, and everything else of organizational capability that supports those employees' productivity—in a word, everything left at the office when the employees go home. Structural capital also includes customer capital, the relationships developed with key customers. Unlike human capital, structural capital can be owned and thereby traded.

HUMAN CAPITAL

+ STRUCTURAL CAPITAL *)

= INTELLECTUAL CAPITAL

*) e.g., IT organizations, customer relationships
i.e., all that is left behind when staff
is going home

It is easy to see why Intellectual Capital does not fit within traditional accounting models. In particular, Intellectual Capital values activities, such as customer loyalty or employee competence building, that may not impact the bottom line of a company for years. And it devalues near-term success that does not position the company for the future.

Intellectual Capital may be a new theory, but in practice it has been around for years as a form of common sense. It has always lurked in that multiple between a company's market value and its book value.[21] But until recently, it was always assumed that this difference was entirely a subjective factor, driven by gossip, insider information about upcoming products, and a gut feeling about a company's prospects, that could never be empirically measured. Moreover, it was also assumed that any such gap was a temporary aberration, a nonempirical added value that would, in due time, manifest itself in some form—increased revenues, reduced overhead, improved productivity or market share—that could be measured by traditional means.

But recent business history has shown neither to be true. The core of the so-called *knowledge economy* is huge investment flows into human capital as well as information technology. And, stunningly, neither of these appear as positive values in traditional accounting. Rather, it is often just the opposite. Yet, these investments are the key tools of the new value creation.

Somehow, if only by hunches and intuitions, the market *is* putting a value on invisible assets. And some of these qualitative assets seem to hover in the ether almost indefinitely, converting to line items on the balance sheet years after the market has accounted for them.

The recognition of this new business reality is forcing a new balance to emerge, in which the past is balanced by the future and the financial by the nonfinancial—Intellectual Capital.

FINDING THE NEW BALANCE

INTELLECTUAL CAPITAL

=

KNOWLEDGE CAPITAL

=

NONFINANCIAL ASSETS

=

IMMATERIAL ASSETS

=

HIDDEN ASSETS

=

INVISIBLE ASSETS

=

MEANS TO ACHIEVE TARGET

=

IC=MV-BV (James Tobin)

The case for establishing a new way to measure institutional value is powerful. If Intellectual Capital represents the buried root mass of the visible tree, or, to use another familiar image, the giant iceberg hidden beneath the tiny islet above the surface; if it indeed accounts for two-thirds or more of the real worth of companies; then we are faced not just with an inequity in the investment community but a true crisis that extends across the economy. Given the frenzied pace of technological change and the almost instantaneous speed of modern telecommunications, we are flying blindly in a hurricane depending on instruments that measure the wrong things. (Some of the latest theories about Intellectual Capital even suggest that it is related to chaos theory or to complex adaptive—that is, living—systems.)

Obviously this imbalance cannot continue. The sheer wasteful-ness of resources flowing to the wrong places at the wrong time is dangerous enough. But an even greater risk is that the same indica-tors that fail to show the economy surging upward are also likely to miss when those underlying forces start trending down. We are in enormous danger of losing our direction and flying straight into the ground without even knowing we are heading toward disaster. This alone should chill the soul of every investor, manager, or politician . . . and it should be more than incentive to search for effective ways to measure and nurture Intellectual Capital.

Not that this search will be easy. By its very definition, subjec-tive information cannot be strictly codified. And this fuzziness courts abuse. Says Herwick, "Whenever money is involved, peo-ple will abuse the process." In particular, he doubts any company will make projections about future intangibles unless they are legally "held harmless and blameless." But that itself may open the door to wild and patently false predictions. "So," says Herwick, "in an attempt to protect the individual investor, we may ironically create a system that allows for greater abuse."[22]

He isn't alone. Davidow, too, fears the scenario of "a company president standing up to announce that 'the company factory has burned down, we've lost all of our significant customers, but thanks to an as-yet unproven scientific breakthrough, we are today announcing major profits.'" Ken Hagerty, who, as director of the Coalition for American Equity Expansion, led the U.S. electronics industry in its battle against government plans for a values-based stock option accounting plan, is equally concerned. "How can you put a value on risk taking?" he asks. "It sounds like the same approach all over again, operating from the same flawed judgement base—and it could lead to the same outcry."[23]

These concerns, coming from industry veterans, cannot be ignored. But neither should they stop the movement toward iden-tifying and measuring Intellectual Capital. The need is simply too great, and the current lack of consensus too costly, to turn back. Certainly the current accounting system has hardly had an uncheckered history. Rather, it has reached an acceptable balance between the thousands of companies that use the system properly and the handful that take advantage of its soft spots—a balance made more acceptable because of the punitive enforcement powers of the SEC. The same, we believe, can be done with Intellectual Capital reporting. The most obvious potential abuses can be checked from the start, the more subtle ones countered by a growing body of statutes and case law.

It is comforting that one individual who believes Intellectual Capital disclosure can and must be done is Steven M. H. Wallman, one of the two current commissioners of the Securities and Exchange Commission. "What seems clear to me is that [an accounting entry of] zero is the wrong answer," he says. "So the question is: how do you appropriately report intellectual capital?"[24]

Wallman admits to sharing the others' fears. Not only, he says, is there the danger of fraud surrounding the measurement of Intellectual Capital, but perhaps even worse, the risk that honest companies will produce these numbers in good faith, then be sued for misrepresentation when the predictions don't pan out.

At the same time, Wallman says, "Disclosure is good for everybody because it reduces risk—and that makes the cost of capital lower for companies, lowers the returns demanded by investors, and in turn benefits everyone else from employees to suppliers." Even accounting firms, he adds, might find the new reporting systems represent an opportunity to market more of their services.

"If we can just come up with the right balance," says Wallman, "everybody wins."[25]

PIONEERING EFFORTS

In July 1994, a pioneering group from industry, academia, and policy research met in Mill Valley near San Francisco to start the search for this "right balance." The gathering began with simple questions:

Does the existing management language value knowledge as an essential resource for creating value and wealth? What are the meaningful predictors of a company's future prosperity? How shall we value and measure intellectual capital?[26]

At the heart of this group's work was the belief that most, if not all, of a company's Intellectual Capital *could* be visualized in some way. In particular, the right empirical indicators could be identified and measured, and the right presentational format found, such that Intellectual Capital could be put on the same strong, objective, and comparative base as financial capital.

The work of this group obviously struck a vast and hidden reservoir of need. By October 1994, *Fortune* magazine carried a cover story on the subject, entitled "Your Company's Most Valuable Asset: Intellectual Capital," that served as a wake-up call to enterprises everywhere that the age of Intellectual Capital had begun.

Tom Stewart, author of the article, observed the emerging IC research efforts and came to his own conclusions:

> Two quick points. First, knowledge may be intangible, but that doesn't mean it can't be measured. Markets do it. Wall Street prices high-tech stocks at a higher premium to book value that it does stocks in industries whose technology is mature. It also reacts, generally with high prices, to announcements of increased R&D spending. Labor markets price knowledge too—for most people, income correlates better with IQ than with the ability to do push-ups.
>
> Second, this isn't just an exercise. The guardians of accounting standards are correct to worry about putting unproven and idiosyncratic data into corporate reports. But the data are vital.[27]

The real breakthrough in Intellectual Capital research came in May 1995 when Skandia, the largest insurance and financial services company in Scandinavia, after several years of internal pioneering work, released the world's first public Intellectual Capital annual report, as a supplement to the financial report.

Skandia had been investigating Intellectual Capital for four years under the leadership of this book's coauthor, Leif Edvinsson. Edvinsson, with the world's first title of corporate director of Intellectual Capital, was also organizer of that pioneering group that had met in Mill Valley. Beginning in 1991, Edvinsson had set out with a team of accounting and finance specialists to develop for Skandia's fast-growing assurance and financial services unit, Skandia AFS, the first-ever organizational structure—a new "accounting taxonomy"[28] they called it—for presenting human capital, structural capital, and the other components of Intellectual Capital.

At the heart of the Skandia IC model was the idea that the true value of a company's performance lies in its ability to create sustainable value by pursuing a business vision and its resulting strategy. From this strategy one could determine certain *success factors* that must be maximized. These success factors could in turn be grouped into four distinct areas of *focus*:

- Financial
- Customer
- Process
- Renewal and development

as well as one commonly shared fifth area:

- Human

Finally, within each of these five areas of focus, one could identify numerous key indicators to measure performance.

Combined, these five factors created a new holistic and dynamic reporting model, which Skandia called the *Navigator*. In the words of Skandia's then-CEO, Bjorn Wolrath:

> Measurement of intellectual capital and a balanced reporting represent an important milestone in the shift from the Industrial

Era into the Knowledge Economy. . . . This broadened, balanced type of accounting and reporting results in a more systematic description of the company's ability and potential to transform intellectual capital into financial capital.[29]

The indicators the Navigator tracked ranged from the commonsensical—fund assets, income per employee, marketing expense per customer—to the unexpected—telephone accessibility, days spent visiting customers, information technology literacy, even laptop computers per employee.

The Skandia 1994 IC Annual Report was a landmark in the story of the standardization of the Intellectual Capital model. But it wasn't the only emerging event. Dow Chemical, for example, created the position of director of intellectual assets, who set out to create an IC report for that company. Hughes Aircraft also set up an Intellectual Capital program called the Knowledge Highway. The Canadian Imperial Bank of Commerce, North America's seventh largest bank, formed its leadership development program around Intellectual Capital, then used those skills to institute a loan program to finance knowledge-based companies using Intellectual Capital valuations as the key criteria. In South Korea, steel giant Posco started its own IC department.

Ernst & Young, the accounting giant, established seminar programs for its clients about Intellectual Capital entitled "New Values and Measurements for the Knowledge Era" and "The Knowledge Advantage." Arthur Andersen developed a collection of Knowledge Assessment Tools for use by its clients. And at several of the large corporations, patent and trademark managers also turned to Intellectual Capital to refine the value extraction of idle intellectual property.

Clearly a movement had begun. Its first phase culminated in a symposium in April 1996 in Washington, D.C., on Intellectual Capital, sponsored by that arbiter of the old accounting model itself, the Securities and Exchange Commission. At that meeting, Commissioner Wallman predicted that Intellectual Capital, and the Skandia supplement approach in particular, would one day become the heart of the modern corporate annual report—to which today's financial statements would be added as appendices. He further advised companies to begin experimenting with the disclosure of hidden assets through published supplements.

In just a few years, Intellectual Capital had jumped from an idea to a working concept to the brink of becoming a new corporate disclosure standard. In the words of knowledge–business theorist Charles Savage[30] and entrepreneur Charles Armstrong:[31]

> In the short space of about three years, we already see an evolution in thinking, from identifying the components of Intellectual Capital to an understanding of the dynamic interaction between these components.[32]

Clearly Intellectual Capital is an idea whose time has come. Common sense is about to be put into common practice.

IMPLEMENTING THE THEORIES

This book is written to be the core text of Intellectual Capital's second era, that of application and capitalization.

Application, because for the rest of this decade and beyond hundreds of thousands of companies, large and small, throughout the world will adopt Intellectual Capital as a way of measuring, visualizing, and presenting the true value of their businesses.

They will do so because Intellectual Capital accounting uniquely recognizes what counts in the modern economy of fast-moving, knowledge-intensive virtual corporations:

- Strong and enduring business relationships within networked partnerships.
- The enduring loyalty of customers.

19

- The role of key employees, upon whose knowledge and competencies the company's future rests.
- The commitment of the company and its employees to learn and renew over time.
- And most of all, the *character* and *values* of a company, a crucial tool for investors and executives when looking at mergers, acquisitions, alliances, personnel hiring, and partnering.

The Skandia Navigator, and the value scheme of IC-components that underlies it, is but the first systematic attempt to uncover these factors and to establish the key indicators for establishing their metrics. There will be others. With trial and error the best of these indicators will emerge as general IC reporting standards.

In the first nine chapters, this book will systematically lay out the underlying philosophy of Intellectual Capital, present some key features of the best management attempts to date, show how it can be done in any company, and warn of potential pitfalls. It will also show that measuring Intellectual Capital is only one of six steps to constructing a value-enhancing and -sustaining organization.

Chapters 5–9 in particular will investigate in turn each of the five IC focus areas in depth, explaining their underlying philosophy and measurement methodology, and then offering sample indicators.

Everything then comes together in chapter 10, as the different focus areas are organized into a unified whole, and two new universal IC measures—the *IC absolute value* and the *IC efficiency coefficient*—are elaborated for the first time. In doing all of this, we hope to bring readers to a common starting point from which they can explore the Intellectual Capital of their own companies—and ultimately play a part in the creation of global IC practices.

Capitalization of the IC model is the subject of the final two chapters. Ultimately, these may prove the most important of all, because Intellectual Capital represents such a fundamentally new way of looking at organizational value that it will never be confined to playing an adjunct role to traditional accounting.

It is human nature to assume that any important new innovation will simply improve upon what preceded it . . . and then to be stunned when it breaks out into new territory of its own. Thus, the march of computers through corporations has been one long story of users trying to confine it to improving existing processes—bookkeeping, manufacturing, management reporting, payroll, sales—only to find that it leads to a radical restructuring of the entire discipline. So it was with the computer, which was supposed to speed up the assembly line; it often got rid of the line altogether, replacing it with mass customization, an impossible notion just a decade before.

So it is with Intellectual Capital. Even among the growing ranks of IC adherents the magnitude of the financial revolution Intellectual Capital represents is often lost. In truth, this new model of measuring value will transform not just the economy but society itself in its wealth creation and value extraction.

How? Because it looks at human and structural factors, not just financial factors, as value creators. Intellectual Capital is not confined strictly to for-profit enterprises. It can also be applied to nonprofits, the military, churches, even governments. The result is the first common yardstick to measure and compare value growth in *every* type of enterprise in a society.

It is difficult to even imagine what this means: Intellectual Capital holds out the possibility of a common valuation of *all* human group endeavors. And that will undoubtedly affect the way we invest, donate, even vote in the future. This common yardstick is the subject of chapter 11.

Finally, any revolution in the way we judge the value of an item also radically affects the way we exchange that item. New categories or new levels of abstraction produce new markets. Thus, just as the agricultural economy produced a secondary market in commodities exchange, and the industrial economy led to the rise of securities and stock exchanges, so too it is likely that the new knowledge-based economy will generate its own unique form of secondary trading. And, just as accounting was and is the underlying measurement system for capital stock, so too intellectual capital will be the system for this new exchange. For now, in chapter 12, we can only speculate what that exchange will be like and how it will operate. But have no doubt: Like its predecessors, this exchange will come to dominate the economic health and wealth of the society it serves.

The rise of Intellectual Capital is inevitable, given the irresistible historical and technological forces, not to mention the investment flows, that are sweeping across the modern world and driving us toward a knowledge economy. Intellectual Capital will come to dominate the way we value our institutions because it alone captures the dynamics of organizational sustainability and value creation. It alone recognizes that a modern enterprise changes so fast that all it has left to depend on is the talents and dedication of its people and the quality of the tools they use.

But most of all, Intellectual Capital is inevitable because it alone, of any model for measuring corporate performance, pierces the surface and uncovers true value. In doing so, it restores both common sense and fairness to economics.

In reading this book you are hearing the first drumbeats of a radical rethinking of the way businesses and institutions see themselves—and how others see them as well. Step lively now and you will be in the vanguard of this movement, better prepared and more experienced than your competitors. Or wait, until it washes over you and tosses you forward, struggling to keep from being dashed and drowned.

But make no mistake, whatever path you choose, Intellectual Capital is our future.

The Hidden Capabilities of a Corporation

What is value?

Generations of business and accounting students have been taught that value lies in *assets*.[1] Assets in turn are everything owned by a company that has money value. Assets come in four forms, three of them precise and measurable, and the fourth imprecise and essentially unmeasurable until it is sold.

The first two types of assets are *current,* meaning they are likely to be consumed or sold within the next year, such as inventories and accounts receivable; and *fixed* (or *long-life*), which, in the form of plant, equipment, and property, have a useful life of more than a year. Fixed assets, because their value is used up in increments over multiple financial reporting periods, are *depreciated,* that is, their cost is spread out in a reasonable and systematic way across successive balance sheets.

The third type of asset is *investments,* such as a company's holdings in stocks and bonds. Though this type of asset is typically more volatile than the first two, it nevertheless can be measured in a systematic way through market value and other metrics.

The fourth asset type, however, is far more problematic. *Intangible assets* are those that have no physical existence but are still of value to the company. Typically they are long term, and just as typically they cannot accurately be valued until the company is sold.

Intangible assets are the boon and bane of accounting. On the one hand the category is an effective catchall for all those corporate assets, evanescent as they may be, that just don't fit into those nicely rigid first three categories. On the other hand, the existence of intangible assets represents a tacit admission by the accounting world that its elegantly tautological core equivalence,

Assets = Liabilities + Capital

that nightmare of bookkeepers at 3:00 A.M. trying to balance the books, does in fact have a built-in fudge factor that grows less empirical and more irrational the closer you look at it.

Intangible assets arose in response to a growing recognition that non-bookkeeping-type factors can have an important role to play in a company's real value. Some of these were pretty obvious: Patents, trademarks, copyrights, exclusive market rights—all conferred on their owners a competitive advantage that had an impact on the bottom line. In some way they were obviously connected to the capital side of the company's assets.

Others seemed to affect the liability side. For example, when a company dedicated years of research and development funds to the development of a new process or technology, that investment, too, ultimately contributed to the value of the company. And a systematic method, comparable to depreciation, called *amortization,* was devised to convert this cost into an expense as the intangible asset was used up.

But even this wasn't enough to capture all the intangible assets of a company. There were other, even less rigorous factors that often only made themselves known when the enterprise was sold. For example, if a business had total assets of $2 million, yet sold for $2.2 million, there had to be something the buyer, assuming he or she wasn't crazy, saw in that company that increased its apparent value, in this case by $200,000.

What is that added value? It might be the loyalty of customers, or the recognition of a business name that had been around for decades, or store location, even the character of the employees. Whatever, these factors were lumped under the title *goodwill,* just as services once were.

Goodwill, as inexplicit as it was, could also be amortized over intervals ranging from five to forty years. Thus, the buyer of that business who paid the extra $200,000 was required to write off that goodwill, whatever its makeup, over the time it would take to enjoy the full benefits of that goodwill, however long that is.

Determining all of this is the job of the buyer and, sometimes, the tax collector.

If all of this seems a little loosey-goosey to you, especially in light of the image of precision and rigor that traditionally accrues to the accounting profession—and if it also seems like an intellectual hole big enough for every crook, con man, and embezzler to drive an armored car through—you are right on both counts. Intangible assets, and especially goodwill, drive the accounting profession crazy . . . and it endlessly struggles to get the subject under control through case and precedent, new standards and government regulations.

Unfortunately for them, as the years go on, the role of these intangibles gets greater and greater, to the point that in some companies it completely overwhelms the tangibles. Witness that up to nine times market valuation of the book value of U.S. companies. At the end of the twentieth century, it would seem that intangible assets have won the day.

THE FASB FIASCO

Still, the accounting profession strives heroically to force these new values into the old suit of clothes. Thus, in 1993, the Financial Accounting Standards Board (FASB), the arbiter of accounting rules that advises the Securities and Exchange Commission, set out to give some sort of reportable value to stock options.

FASB's logic was unassailable. New start-up companies often substitute founders' stock for salary as a lure to industry veterans to join the entrepreneurial team. Thus, a division general manager of a billion-dollar manufacturer might take a 50 percent pay cut in order to earn options on a half million shares of stock at fifty cents per share as CEO of a brand-new firm with six employees and no sales expected for several years.

Then, as sometimes happens in places like Silicon Valley, that little company finally introduces a product and sees its revenues skyrocket. And when it decides to have its initial public offering of stock, that executive's shares jump in value from fifty cents to $35, literally in the course of a single morning. He has just made $35 million—or at least will when he exercises his options. Yet, until that moment, the company's books have shown his options as worth $250,000.

FASB, which is chartered to protect investors by enforcing full disclosure, didn't like this at all. Neither did big public corporations, which felt that the little start-ups were enjoying an unfair reporting advantage. Certain Democratic congressmen were angry too, believing such stock option plans were yet another subterfuge to make the rich even richer.

So FASB, as was its normal procedure, announced a series of hearings and meetings to discuss new rules for the formal reporting of stock options. Part of this process was for governors and employees of the board to hold hearings around the country to allow alternative views on the subject to be aired.

FASB never knew what hit it. When FASB chairman Dennis R. Beresford and his team held a hearing in San Jose, California, they nearly found themselves the target of a lynch mob. One corporate executive after another got up and denounced the proposal. Major industry groups, such as the American Electronics Association, denounced the proposal as well. And in Congress, both GOP and Democratic lawmakers filed bills to stop the plan—and even talked about eliminating FASB itself as an adviser to the SEC.

FASB, feeling for its very existence, backed off.

In retrospect, a lot of these complaints by industry were obviously self-serving, designed to escape more taxes and government red tape, while keeping a great recruiting tool. But there was also an element of realism in those complaints. It was this realism that FASB, for all of its talk about rational reporting, obviously missed, and one that points away from the traditional philosophy of accounting and toward an Intellectual Capital model.

What those angry Silicon Valley CEOs were intuitively objecting to was what might be characterized as a misguided attempt to turn a philosophy into an accounting entry.

How so? Well, consider the idea of "founders stock." In the words of Valley pioneer Al Shugart, it "is the mother's milk of Silicon Valley." The Valley had become one of the most dynamic entrepreneurial communities in history largely because it had created an environment in which workers willingly traded the predictability of salaries for the chance to strike it rich through stock options. In established companies, this translated into employee stock participation that often reached 100 percent, the greatest such involvement on the planet. In new start-up companies it meant heavy sacrifices for the long shot of becoming a tycoon—a payoff that occurred just often enough in the Valley to make everybody else a believer.

Thus, in Silicon Valley, FASB managed the neat trick of angering two often opposing constituencies. The established companies were mad because they felt they were going to be punished for being more democratic and more equitable with their employees than their counterparts elsewhere.

And the start-ups were angry because they rightly saw themselves being saddled with a taxable asset that was no more accurately valued with the FASB measure than the one they were using. Sure, that fifty cents per share founders stock *might* turn into a hundred bucks per share someday—but, given that nine out of ten start-up companies died, it was far more likely to turn out worth *zero*. In trying to not miss that one jackpot, FASB was willing to ignore the nine other times when even the lower valuation was inflated.

But it went even deeper than that, and that is the point of recalling FASB's fiasco. The new world of business is built on tenets, rules, and equations that are often different from those that came before. Silicon Valley, for example, as Tom Peters has often noted, appears to be the story of success, but it is, in fact, built on failure. For every Netscape, Oracle, or Cisco, there are scores of other companies with similar dreams and comparable products that, for one reason or another, failed. Thanks to the migratory nature of the Valley's worker population, the lessons of these failures are quickly disseminated and assimilated throughout the Valley, becoming the foundation of shared value creation knowledge upon which the successful companies are built.

Maintaining such a fragile business environment requires a carefully tended system of rewards and motivators. Thus, unlike most industries, the punishment for failure in Silicon Valley is typically almost nonexistent. In fact, entrepreneurs are often rewarded for failure—venture capitalists prefer to see such "seasoning" among the executives in the companies in which they invest. Conversely, the commitment of time and energy is so great in a new start-up company, and the chances of success so slim even in a place like Silicon Valley, that the payoff must be very big for the small minority of winners. You need a few billionaires like Steve Jobs and Larry Ellison to put stars in the eyes of the hundreds that emulate them, and since no salary could ever be sufficient, the only way to create the potential for a huge reward is through options on founders stock.

For those reasons, ingrained as the system was into the daily working world of the high-tech industry, Silicon Valley's leaders understood the vital need not to mess with its stock options. FASB, concerned first and foremost with bookkeeping accuracy, missed the point entirely. Had it implemented FASB's original plans, the SEC might well have decapitated the most productive sector in the U.S. economy. Instead, it appeared to learn its lesson and started a research program into intangible assets.

The stock option story is but one example of how traditional models of financial value are increasingly clashing with evolving business notions of competitive value. If stock options were the only ground for dispute, no doubt some accommodation might be reached to preserve the supremacy of the financial accounting model. But you need only peruse the business shelves of your local bookstore to quickly appreciate how quickly that model and real-life, progressive business practices are starting to diverge.

Take, for example, in very brief summaries, what some of the leading business gurus are saying it takes for a business to successfully compete.

Peter Drucker. Innovation is the core competence of the competitive modern enterprise. It must be established at the heart of the organization from the beginning, continuously nurtured by investment and executive support, and it must be systematically transformed into value for the firm.

Dee Hock. We are currently in an era of institutional failure, where the old value system and the traditional organization forms no longer work. What are now needed are "chaordic" (organized chaotic) organizations that value speed, flexibility, and adaptability.

Andrew Grove Companies must be ever watchful, to the point of paranoia, for sudden, technology-driven, categorical transformations that threaten not only their products but the very way they do business.

Tom Peters. In a world of rapid, even explosive, change, companies must construct a comparably dynamic organization that enlists customers, employees, and strategic partners in pursuit of relationships, products, and work environments that create high excitement, creativity, and satisfaction.

Jerry Porras and James Collins. Older, established companies can not only find a place in the new economy, but even lead it, if they have established a powerful corporate philosophy based upon the company's stories and legends and that is used to imbue each employee with a model of behavior aligned with that philosophy.

Michael Porter. The competitive health of a company is a function of the combination of the strength, energy, and competence of its suppliers, customers, current competitors, and potential competitors—the last including, most dangerously, unanticipated competitors from an entirely different field who offer a new substitute product category.

That's just a half dozen of the best-known current business thinkers. The reader can likely add twice that many more from his or her own reading.

What is important about this list is that these are ideas being applied today in thousands of companies throughout the world, yet *none* of them are readily transferable to the balance sheet.

Actually, that's not quite true: To implement many of them would in fact hurt the company's books in the short term thanks to the cost of reorganization, buying MIS equipment, improving customer service systems, putting in place electronic data interchange systems with suppliers, establishing a strategic planning operation, and so on. Down the line these actions may make the company's books look rosy indeed, but for the near term they make those same books appear weak against shortsighted competitors who maintain the status quo—and that in turn will compromise that company's ability to obtain capital. Simply put, the smart, forward-looking company is punished for trying to maintain its competitiveness and earnings capability.

Ultimately what this means is that the traditional accounting model not only acts as a de facto obstacle to the dissemination of a company's real story but ultimately retards the entire economy's ability to maintain its competitiveness in a rapidly changing environment. When a company's only hope for a fair valuation comes down to convincing shareholders (by first convincing analysts) to ignore quarterly earnings in light of the company's long-term infrastructure investments, we are in a world turned upside down . . . a sensation that is increasingly being felt by today's business executives, shareholders, and investors.

NARINGSLIV

What, then, should we value? What perspective shall we take? Certainly revenues, profits, and earnings cannot be ignored. They are the ultimate measure of a company's success. They must remain the end, if no longer the beginning, of all corporate value measurements.

But what else counts? And how do these factors interrelate among themselves and with a company's financial structure?

One useful way to look at a company (or, as we shall see, any organization) is as a tree. The trunk, branches, and leaves, the parts of the tree visible to the observer, are the company as it is known to the marketplace and is what is expressed by the accounting process. The fruit produced by this tree is the profits and products harvested by investors and consumed by customers.

The hidden value of a company is the root system of that tree. And for that tree to flourish and bear fruit, the tree must be nourished by strong and healthy roots. And just as the quality of a tree's fruit is dependent upon its root system, so too the quality of a company's business organization and the strength of its financial capital is a function of its hidden values. Nurture these roots and the company flourishes; allow them to wither or become damaged and the company, no matter how strong it looks, will eventually topple and die.

This is not a new discovery. Observers have always incorporated a subjective measure of hidden values into any analysis of a company's value. The difference is, to return to our analogy, if the visible part of the tree is healthy and the environment unchanging, you can pretty much assume the parts of the tree you can't see—the roots—are healthy as well. Only occasionally do you get surprised by an apparently healthy tree that is rotten at the core.

But when the climate is in flux, when predators and parasites are everywhere, understanding what takes place underground suddenly becomes more important than what is going on above. Strong roots may be the only thing that gets a tree through an unexpected drought or freeze.

So it is with companies. As the saying goes, watch out for old oaks: They may appear formidable but are rotted away at their core and waiting to fall over in the first storm. In companies this hollowing is usually intentional. It is the inevitable behavior of

INTELLECTUAL CAPITAL

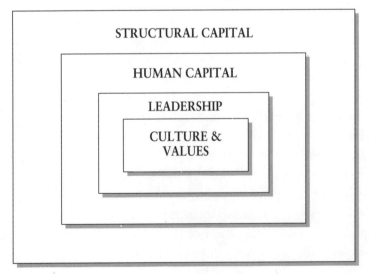

managers who are rewarded for cost-cutting and who respond by cutting away not only deadwood but heartwood.

In an era of rapid technological change, when entire product categories can disappear overnight, when competition can come from unexpected directions, and new types of relationships are being forged between suppliers, manufacturers, and customers—i.e., when all of the predictions of those visionaries listed earlier are suddenly coming true—these core values and competencies of a company may be not only what keeps it alive but the only part of the company left to emerge on the other side.

It is interesting to note that whereas the English term "business" seems to connote, among other things, the "busyness" of frenzied, often undirected activity, the Swedish counterpart is *naringsliv*, which literally translates as "nourishment for life." That's not a bad perspective for the new organization.

Consider the story of Lotus. Lotus, founded in 1980, made its name as a leading supplier of personal computer software, notably spreadsheets. This business had made Lotus rich, but it also drew a host of competitors, notably giant Microsoft. So, though its balance sheet was good, the company was increasingly weak and vulnerable to outside competition. Thus, the company's apparent value, measured by its balance sheet, remained high, while its true value, measured by its Intellectual Capital, was plummeting.

Then, an interesting thing happened. The tables turned. In the approving words of one observer, business legend Andrew Grove:

> But while this was happening, Lotus had developed a new generation of software, embodied in [its] product Notes, that promised to bring the same kind of productivity gains to groups that spreadsheets had brought to individuals. Even as Lotus was struggling with spreadsheets and its related software business, its management committed itself to group computing to the extent of de-emphasizing their spreadsheet business. It continued to invest in developing Notes throughout those difficult years and it mounted a major marketing and development program that suffused all the corporate statements.[2]

In other words, just when Lotus looked the strongest, it was weakest, and when it looked the weakest, thanks to its intangible assets, it may have been strongest.

The result, when the company was taken over by IBM in 1995: Lotus was valued at fifteen times its published book value because of its millions of customers, intensive research and development, strong market position, and brand name—especially that of Notes. IBM paid $3.5 billion for a company that on paper was worth only $230 million. Why? Because of the other assets, such as customer bases, staff knowledge, and most of all, for the type of software innovation that could create a Notes and a management astute enough to bet a whole company on it.[3]

CAPITAL FORMS

What are these hidden values? They appear to take three basic forms: human capital, structural capital, and customer capital.

Human Capital

All individual capabilities, the knowledge, skill, and experience of the company's employees and managers, is included under the term human capital. But it must be more than simply the sum of these measures; rather, it also must capture the dynamics of an intelligent organization in a changing competitive environment. For example: Are employees and managers constantly upgrading their skills and adding new ones? Are these new skills and competencies recognized by the company and incorporated into its operations? And are these new skills, as well as the experiences of company veterans, being shared throughout the organization? Or, alternatively, is the company still drawing on a body of aging and increasingly obsolete skills, ignoring (even punishing) new competencies gained by employees, and locking up knowledge as a way of cornering power and influence within the organization?

Human capital also must include the creativity and innovativeness of the organization. How often are new ideas generated in-house? How often are those ideas implemented? And what is the ratio of their success?[4]

Structural Capital

Structural capital might best be described as the embodiment, empowerment, and supportive infrastructure of human capital. It is also the organizational capability, including the physical systems used to transmit and store intellectual material. According to Hubert Saint-Onge, former vice president of learning organization and leadership development at Canadian Imperial Bank of Commerce (CIBC), now VP, People, Knowledge & Strategies at the Mutual Life of Canada, and also a leading theory developer of Intellectual Capital, the relationship between human and structural capital is a "double-arrow dynamic." In Saint-Onge's words, "Human capital is what builds structural capital, but the better your structural capital, the better your human capital is likely to be."[5]

It includes such factors as the quality and reach of information technology systems, company images, proprietary databases, organizational concepts, and documentation. Here, too, can also be found, like a reminder of the world left behind, traditional items such as intellectual properties including patents, trademarks, and copyrights.

Needless to say, this is a lot of diverse components. One way to organize it is to see structural capital as itself composed of three types of capital: organizational, innovation, and process. *Organizational capital* is the company's investment in systems, tools, and operating philosophy that speeds the flow of knowledge through the organization, as well as out to the supply and distribution channels. It is the systemized, packaged, and codified competence of the organization as well as the systems for leveraging that capability. *Innovation capital* refers to the renewal capability and the results of innovation in the form of protected commercial rights, intellectual property, and other intangible assets and talents used to create and rapidly bring to market new products and services. *Process capital* is those work processes, techniques (such as ISO 9000), and employee programs that augment and enhance the efficiency of manufacturing or the delivery of services. It is the kind of practical knowledge used in continuous value creation.

Subsumed under innovation capital are the two traditional nonphysical assets: *intellectual properties* (such as trademarks) and the surviving residue of *intangible assets,* such as the theory by which the business is run. Here, one might say, we are at the very root tips of the tree.[6]

Customer Capital

The original Skandia model places the valuation of customer relationships under structural capital. But it is interesting to note that in a recently developed IC model, refined by Saint-Onge at CIBC,[7] customer capital is broken out as a separate category, equivalent to structural and human capital.[8] It is an interesting idea, suggesting both that the relationship of a company to its customers is distinct from that of its dealings with employees and strategic partners, and that this relationship is of absolutely central importance to the company's worth. Time will tell whether this distinction is intrinsically valid or merely a means to promote the company to investors and to motivate employees and other stakeholders.[9]

Customer capital would have been a truly alien notion to bookkeepers just a few decades ago. Yet it has always been there, hidden within the entry for "goodwill." After all, when a company sells for more than book value, after you subtract away the value of patents and copyrights, what else is that difference but a recognition that the company has a strong and loyal customer base?[10]

Saint-Onge argues "that the bank's relationships with [its customers] have a value, which any potential purchaser of the bank would have to pay for."[11] We'll go even further: The customer relationship is where cash flow starts, not in the accounting department, despite what many managers seem to think.

Measuring that strength and loyalty is the challenge for the customer capital category. Indices include measures of satisfaction, longevity, price sensitivity, even the financial well-being of long-term customers.[12]

Together, these three new forms of capital measurement capture a company in motion as it transforms its skills and knowledge into competitiveness and wealth.[13] At Skandia, the initial catchphrase for the project, playing off the new European Currency Unit (ECU), was "IQ to ECU." A more universal and philosophical phrase might be:

"Values to Value."

It also sounds easy, but the jump from theory to practice for Intellectual Capital is a long one. And determining the right indicators and indices to measure may be the easier part of the job.

Far harder may be the task of overcoming institutional inertia. As Saint-Onge has said:

> It's not for the conceptually faint-hearted. Although intangible and often hidden to management, intellectual capital is essential to the long term prosperity of organizations in the knowledge era.
>
> Organizations have been built and run to function in the relatively stable and predictable environment provided by the industrial era. As a result, the current speed of organization renewal is too slow to cope with the velocity of change brought about in the marketplace by the knowledge era.[14]

But the fact the world has changed may not be enough to convince the management and financial accounting staffs of certain companies to keep up with it.

Every company in the world has been organized along the punishment and rewards offered by the traditional financial accounting model. Thus, some companies will likely jump on the IC model because it recognizes assets for which they have not been rewarded before. But other companies will, correctly, realize that the new IC reporting exposes heretofore hidden weaknesses in their businesses that were masked by the good news on the balance sheet. They will resist such change.

That same institutional resistance may also appear in entire industries, as the prospect of rethinking their entire value system paralyzes the companies within it. For example, at Standard Chartered, a British financial institution, head of investor relations Stuart Anderson has been quoted as saying—counter to Saint-Onge, and one might say, with unconscious self-disclosure—that

> IC tends to be more prevalent in high tech companies where the skills and expertise of directors are the only assets a company has. But in the financial sector staff mobility is so high, that I imagine it would be one of the least favorable places for putting intellectual capital on the books.[15]

Finally, there can even be inertia at the national level. For example, even the fairly standardized notion of goodwill is currently a matter of heated debate by the standardizers at the European Union. As it turns out, the United Kingdom, Denmark, Ireland, Italy, and the Netherlands allow goodwill to be written off against reserves on acquisition (as it is in the United States and Canada); but that same practice is illegal in Belgium, Spain, and Portugal. And if a topic as circumscribed as goodwill can provoke such disputation, what will be the likely effect of a wholly new reporting and disclosing system?

Revolutionary, of course. But we already know that. Still, after all the shouting has died down and the resistance overcome, Intellectual Capital will be the new standard. Why? Because it represents *opportunity*. As knowledge organization theorist Karl-

Erik Sveiby has written: "The economy of the Knowledge Era offers unlimited resources, because the human capacity to create knowledge is infinite."[16] Who can walk away from that?

The challenge, then, is to make sure that it is worthy of this important role. That means it must accomplish what it set out to do: capture the true value of an organization. And to do that, any report of Intellectual Capital must be a living, dynamic, *human* document. It must not only have the relevant indicators but also present those measures in a manner that is intuitively understandable, applicable, and even comparable between diverse enterprises.

Most of all, such reporting must be useful in real-life applications. That is, even if it is not yet the perfect solution, it is along the path toward that solution. It is better to be roughly right than to be precisely wrong.

One might object that the current standard, financial accounting, barely fulfills the requirement of intuitiveness. And certainly, many of its more recondite categories are gibberish to the average person. Nevertheless, in the five centuries since the creation of double-entry bookkeeping, accounting has developed a language, grammar, and vocabulary that is taught to and used daily by millions.

Intellectual Capital doesn't have the luxury of a half millennium to let the world adapt to it; rather, it must go more than halfway to meet its audience. The first-time reader of an Intellectual Capital report must come away with a broader perspective of its messages. No mere list of measurements, no matter how artfully phrased, will meet such a requirement. Rather, these measures must be placed into a larger structure—a format, a navigational tool—that will bring them all together to produce a comprehensive and overarching meaning about sustainability and future earnings capability.

Such a format, called the Business Navigator, has already been devised and put to use by Skandia. How the Navigator works will be described in chapter 4. In the meantime, let's look at the history of how Skandia came to design it.

Finding Its Way

What drives a company to look beyond the balance sheet to new ways of measuring the value of its own operations?

For Skandia, the process began already in the 1980s when the company's then-CEO, Bjorn Wolrath, and the now first executive vice president of Skandia as well as head of Skandia AFS, Jan Carendi, began to see how traditional management theory just didn't seem to fit anymore with the development of service business, especially those that were knowledge intensive.

Like many other industry leaders throughout the world, both men recognized that a company's competitive strength lay less and less with the traditional accounting assets—buildings, equipment, inventories—than with a number of new factors, like individual talent, synergistic market relationships, and the ability to manage the flow of competence. They realized that if they could just get their hands around these new intangibles, develop ways to grow them, and measure them, they might just have, in Wolrath's words, "a new, holistic and more balanced set of tools for growing Skandia."

But how would you ever measure such intangible factors? The number of new services launched? The number of nodes in a company's information network? Work processes? The number of successful customers? The number of new ideas being generated by employees each month? It all seemed just too ineffable to ever pull down onto a printed page.

Even in Sweden, Skandia wasn't alone in its frustration. Founded in the early 1980s by Wolworth and Edvinsson among others, the Swedish Coalition of Service Industries had been focusing the problem of visualizing true value of the service sector. In 1985, the coalition's very first publication focused upon service development and highlighted the urgent need for a new approach.

This first publication led to a series of reports, culminating in 1992 with a report on how to value service organizations.[1] This new booklet raised the possibility of a new management approach that emphasized the development and nurturing of service companies' nonfinancial elements.

The first step in Skandia was to create a new corporate position. "I was convinced," says Carendi, "that we needed an Intellectual Capital function that was the equivalent of our existing functions, such as Finance and Marketing." In September 1991 Skandia AFS organized the very first corporate Intellectual Capital function— and recruited Leif Edvinsson as its director.

The charter of this new Skandia AFS IC function was to grow and develop the company's Intellectual Capital as a visible, lasting value that would complement the balance sheet. The operation was also to forge a link between other company functions, such as business development, human resources, and information technology. In the process, it was to develop new measurement tools and metrics as well as implement new programs to speed knowledge sharing in the organization.

Says Edvinsson, "I had long been struck by the essential paradox of modern business investment: that if a company invests in those things that will make it competitive, like human capital and information technology, it will suffer a short-term deterioration of its profit and loss statement, which in turn reduces the value of the balance sheet, thereby reducing the book value of the organization. In other words, the more the modern company invests in its future, the less its book value.

"This is absurd. We needed another value-mapping system."

Edvinsson's opinion was only underscored in his mind by the

growing divergence between market and book valuations. There was also support in statements like that of Swedish stock analyst B. Svensson of Dagens Industri that "the stars of the stock exchange attract more with their knowledge than with their substance."

Throughout 1992, Edvinsson assembled his first of several virtual teams and set to work defining the basic character of Intellectual Capital.[2] From this emerged three fundamental insights:

1. Intellectual Capital is supplementary, not subordinate, information to financial information.
2. Intellectual Capital is nonfinancial capital, and represents the hidden gap between market value and book value.
3. Intellectual Capital is a debt issue, not an asset issue.

The third insight was of particular importance, as it meant Intellectual Capital is a debt issue to be regarded in the same way as equity; and that it is borrowed from the stakeholders, that is, customers, employees, and so forth.

The counterbalance to this debt, according to traditional

INTELLECTUAL CAPITAL

	ASSETS	DEBT EQUITY	"Official Bal. Sheet"
"Intellect. Properties"	"Goodwill" "Technology" "Competence"	"Intellectual Capital"	"Hidden Values"

accounting rules, is goodwill. But, by those same rules, goodwill is a trash item, to be deducted as quickly as possible. That, in turn, reduces the value of the balance sheet—the antithesis of the idea of corporate value growing its future.

More than anything else, this failure of the traditional measure of goodwill convinced the Skandia AFS team of the importance of bringing a company's hidden values to the surface where their long-term effects could be made evident.

The next step was to develop a preliminary definition of Intellectual Capital itself. This was the result:

Intellectual Capital is the possession of the knowledge, applied experience, organizational technology, customer relationships and professional skills that provide Skandia with a competitive edge in the market.

It followed, then, that the *value* of Intellectual Capital was the extent to which these intangible assets could be converted into financial returns for the company.

The business division within Skandia pioneering for the first IC measurement was AFS, which developed and administered long-term savings products through a global organizational federation of independent agents such as bankers and brokers. The funds developed by Skandia AFS were managed by alliances with fifty top company managers located throughout the world; were distributed through more than 26,000 brokers and 10,000 bank offices; and served more than 500,000 contracts. The division itself, employing now around 2,000 people, had seen a premium growth from a standing start in the late 1980s to more than 4 billion USD eight years later—and this growth was accelerating.

Thus, AFS was a perfect subject for the test: a global operation moving fast and making its mark through a combination of talented people, innovative products and services, and an increasingly virtual (or in Skandia's term, a "federative networking") organization . . . in other words, through the application of Intellectual Capital.

The IC function set the following goals for its work at AFS:

1. To identify and enhance the visibility and measurability of intangible and soft assets.
2. To capture and support packaging and accessibility by knowledge-sharing technology.
3. To cultivate and channel Intellectual Capital through professional development, training, and IT networking.
4. To capitalize and leverage by adding value through faster recycling of knowledge and increased commercialized transfer of skills and applied expertise.

To this list, Skandia AFS CEO Carendi added that the IC team was to work toward rapidly integrating this newly identified corporate knowledge into tangible assets and enable AFS to apply those assets with maximum competitive effect. Simply put, Carendi wanted AFS turned into an intelligent organization, one that not only learned new skills and taught them to its people but worked to reduce the interval between the two (in Dee Hock's phrase, the "organizational float") to the shortest time possible.

By the middle of 1992, the IC team had begun an inventory of the hidden values of AFS. This led to a very long list of items that were valuable but not disclosed by the accounting system. It included such items as trademarks, concessions, customer databases, fund management systems, IT systems, core competencies, key employees, partners, and alliances. The list exceeded fifty items ... too many and too unwieldy. So, the list was simplified to just two dimensions containing a total of just two dozen indicators.

Ironically, in the meantime, all of this complexity led to a simplified definition:

Human Capital + Structural Capital = Intellectual Capital

In support of this equation was the insight gained by AFS as it had opened new operating units throughout the world. The new emerging units, the IC team realized, mainly represented human capital. By comparison, those which had already been in operation in a market for a length of time had something else, some other factor that went beyond the human factor. Whatever this other factor was, it remained behind when the staff went home for the night. Edvinsson dubbed it *structural capital* and determined that it included the customer database, the concession, the information system, and so on.

There was also another defining characteristic of structural capital: It grew out of human capital. The tree metaphor for Intellectual Capital (as described in the previous chapter) was adopted earlier by the team, and it was found that it could be extended to another discovery: Human capital was the heartwood of the tree, the source of its life. But every year, an organization adds something beyond the staff that, like the rings of a tree, add more strength and durability. These rings are living, vital material too, so just as the tree grows upward and outward, so, too, the role of leadership is the transformation of human capital into structural capital to add to the organization's strength.

Another breakthrough came when the team recognized that whereas human capital cannot be owned, but only rented, structural capital can, from a shareholder's point of view, be owned or traded. Human capital is more volatile, while structural capital is comparatively stable and thus can be used as leverage for financing corporate growth. That's why banks, venture capitalists, and others are more interested in structural capital—though the shrewd ones understand that without strong underlying human capital, any amount of structural capital is all but worthless.

Unfortunately, neither human capital nor structural capital is visible in the traditional accounting system. So that's where the IC team went next, in search of a reporting system that would accurately capture and present these two quantities in a useful form.

But before the work could continue, the program faced one deep philosophical question that conceivably would determine everything thereafter. It was whether the measurement model they created would be designed for valuation or for navigation, that is, comprehensibility.

Had they chosen either path, the subsequent story of Intellectual Capital may have been much different. Instead, returning to Wolrath's original goal of a "holistic and balanced" model, Skandia chose to do both—an example of what is now called *quantum leadership*. It was a big challenge, one that might have resulted in disaster—or at least in a mess of unconnected data—but this time it worked. Valuation and navigation turned out to be two sides of the same coin.

FIRST MESSAGES FROM THE FRONT

As initially planned, the Skandia IC reporting scheme would have six parts and one requirement. The six parts were separate reports on customer development, distribution development, structural development, human development, IT development, and innovation development. The one requirement was to keep it to a single-page format that combined financial and nonfinancial metrics in a simple, intuitive summary.

It proved to be an unrealistic combination—too much information crammed into a small space—but not so unworkable that the team couldn't create just such a one-page report for presentation to the Skandia AFS board in spring 1993. The reception was enthusiastic. AFS CEO Carendi told the team, "This is what the board's been looking for for a long time." But the board also confirmed the team's own opinion when it asked for more insightful information.

But that new request created its own set of problems. The completion of the first report had been a part-time project led by Edvinsson and AFS's deputy controller, Ake Freij. Now they needed help: someone who could assume a full-time control position for IC reporting. In late 1993, Elisabeth Gemzell-Mikkelsen was hired as the world's first IC controller. Others soon followed, creating a team that members joked served as a tent within the Palace of Accounting.

Meanwhile, the situation was far from static inside Skandia itself. The dynamics of AFS were forcing the need for IC reporting even as the team was trying to develop the model for it.

Skandia AFS, along with many of its competitors, had come to realize that to grow as fast as its global markets, the traditional strategy of establishing new subsidiaries abroad was simply too slow and inefficient. Instead, the company embarked on a program of leveraging its internal resources by establishing business alliances with other firms in those regions. The concept was called a *federative organization*, and the goal was to turn Skandia into a true virtual corporation, a collection of "specialists in cooperation."

In such a scenario, the energy of the organization emerges from the autonomy of its satellites. But it only works not only if knowledge is shared within this new metaorganization but if the time between the reception of that information and its application—the "organizational float" again—is perpetually reduced. And so, once again, we are back to Intellectual Capital as the centerpiece of competitiveness.

To its credit, the management of Skandia AFS recognized this, and it formally established as its three building blocks for growing an intelligent organization:

- Technologies
- Values
- Intellectual Capital

For the first time, IC had become part of the core business strategy of an organization.[3]

Just in time, too. The Skandia AFS federation exploded. In 1991 the number of its alliances was about 5,000. Three years later it was 25,000. By 1995 it was almost 50,000. During the same interval, the number of Skandia AFS employees grew from 1,100 to 1,700.

Needless to say, all of this was very good news for Skandia AFS. After all, certain key benefits accrue from this type of design. For one thing, a federative structure requires far less working capital than a collection of subsidiaries. Another benefit, as already noted, is the energy of autonomous units and the experimentation with different policies and methods that might yield more effective and innovative ways of doing business. Third, the two types of capital are organized in the most efficient way: Structural capital is globalized, while human capital is localized.

All well and good. But too many companies pursuing this new organizational model overlook that it also inevitably transforms them internally as well. For example, with a virtual staff scattered throughout the world reporting to their own companies, the traditional head office must also become the "heart office," establishing a business philosophy and operating styles, cultivating allegiance, behavioral values, and ethics, and doing everything else necessary to maintain the cohesion of the larger enterprise. Companies that forget this often find themselves with a virtual corporation tearing itself back into its original pieces. The implication is that the core should reenergize the whole system with values.

However, the growth of alliances is very much invisible from an organizational reporting standpoint. What is seen is the 2,000 current employees but not the leveraging resources of the 65,000 alliances—a thirty-times impact per employee.

One message that came out of this was the need, somewhere in the IC reporting, to recognize and report this ratio of employees to alliances, and thus the leverage of the organization's structural capital. The other was that the traditional corporate human resources function needed to become more externalized in its focus.

But the biggest lesson that emerged from this change in

AFS FEDERATION ENERGETICS

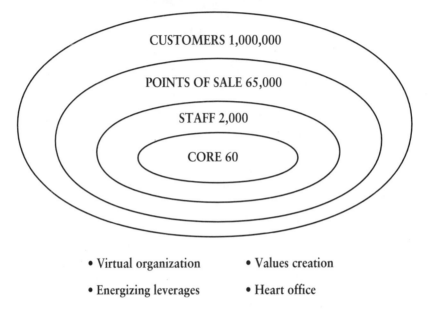

- Virtual organization
- Energizing leverages
- Values creation
- Heart office

Skandia AFS's business organization was that it was no longer enough to simply report the nontangible assets of the company as an ad hoc side document. Now these measurements had to move to the forefront; they had to be integrated into the very corpus of documents that defined the company. And the presence of this new document in that corpus demanded a whole new informational model, a new taxonomy, for the organization.

The debate over the nature of this new taxonomy and how to turn it into a language of numbers and metrics galvanized Skandia during 1994. It was this work that *Fortune* captured in its cover story on Intellectual Capital and Skandia AFS that appeared in October of that year. In fact, by the time the article appeared, Skandia had settled upon its new navigation and reporting schemes.

One interesting feature of this scheme was the choice to do the reporting in numbers. This was not an easy decision, though it may appear so in retrospect. From the start, it was obvious that

Intellectual Capital would be dealing with subjective, even irrational factors, some of which would resist any attempts to translate them into an empirical measure.

So one very appealing possibility was to do this reporting anecdotally; that is, to explain Skandia's IC valuation as a narrative. This would have the advantage of capturing a number of subtleties that would never fit in a table or chart.

But the IC team quickly concluded that the disadvantages of using a narrative (or a strictly graphic) presentation were even greater. For one thing, numbers are the currency of international business. For another, a narrative form would doom IC reporting to traveling the same path as the problem—footnotes and appendices to financial documents—it was partly designed to fix.

Finally, as the IC team only discovered in practice, reporting with numbers also can make information more tangible and dynamic. For example, to report that a customer database is large doesn't do much for the reader. But to report that the customer database has grown by, say, 40 percent over the last twelve months, is a piece of information that can be contemplated, compared with the company's past performance, and matched against the performance of competitors as benchmarking.

So numbers it would be, though the IC team realized that such a decision would require the loss of some of the shadings and colorations of real life that, in a perfect world, would be part of total Intellectual Capital measurement.

Emerging also was this value scheme illustrated in the accompanying diagram as a reminder that there are a number of building blocks adding to the nonfinancial values of a corporation and creating that notorious gap between book value and market value. It also marked the return to importance of the traditional "intellectual" component of corporate valuation: intellectual properties. In its hunt for undiscovered new nontangible assets, the IC team had put aside intellectual property—the legally protected knowledge component of a company, such as patents—as a secondary, and well-established, factor.

But when Skandia AFS grew globally, the issue of IP came roaring back. After all, even the World Trade Organization had organized into three bodies: trade in goods, trade in services, and trade in intellectual properties. And with the biggest international commercial disputes arising over patent and copyright infringements, it was a topic that should be highlighted.

SKANDIA MARKET VALUE SCHEME

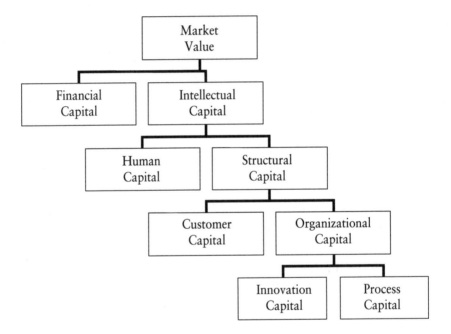

BUILDING AN IC REPORT

All of the pieces were now in place. After internal testing within Skandia AFS, it was now time for the real test: a complete and public IC report for Skandia as a group.

The work began in late 1994, and by May the document was published and distributed to shareholders at the annual meeting.

It was entitled *Visualizing Intellectual Capital,* and was intended as a supplement to the 1994 Skandia Annual Report. It was unlike anything the business world had ever seen, with unusual new measurement schemes, color codes, even a cover that featured the close-up photoimage of a poppy flower, a motif repeated throughout the publication alongside equally rich pictures of sextants and other navigational tools.

This visual scheme was intentional: The break from traditional corporate imagery paralleled the report's break from traditional accounting. It was also a metaphor. As the report noted, "The flowers and navigational tools were chosen to illustrate two important factors in developing intellectual capital: to stimulate growth and renewal, and to always have a clear sense of location and direction."

Visualizing Intellectual Capital was the first public IC annual report, but it was not the first such report for Skandia. An internal document designed to test the opportunity for a "balanced" annual report—that is, a balance between financial and nonfinancial reporting—had been created for internal Skandia use in early 1994. It has also been limited to only Skandia AFS.

But it proved its case, and Skandia commissioned from the team the bigger, companywide document for public distribution and to begin the process of internal benchmarking. In accepting the job, the team had to compromise: As a supplement, the information in *Visualizing Intellectual Capital* was to remain unintegrated with, and subordinate to, the financial summaries of the main report.

Still, it was a start—and a big one. *Visualizing Intellectual Capital* sent shock waves around the world. Within months of its appearance, Edvinsson had been contacted by more than five hundred companies wanting to know how to duplicate the publication. Conferences on Intellectual Capital were convened in London, Brussels, Boston, Houston, Tel Aviv, Toronto, and Caracas. It all culminated in the SEC-sponsored symposium on Intangibles in Washington in April 1996.

By then Skandia had pushed the process even further along. Six months after *Visualizing* the company published an interim report focusing on one of the IC Navigator's areas of focus, *Renewal and Development.* During the spring of 1996, the supplement to the 1995 annual report was published as *Value Creating Processes,* with special attention to growth organization capital. After the conference, during early autumn 1996, the supplement to the 1996 interim report appeared as *Power of Innovation,* emphasizing the roots of renewal and sustainability.

MARKING THE TRAIL

Measuring intangible assets and putting out reports weren't the only activities of the IC function during this period. Another activity was looking back and determining just how they had gotten to this point and what lessons they could learn from the process. These experiences were, after all, yet another intellectual asset of Skandia.

Ultimately, this review involved not only archiving the work of the IC team but also looking at what Skandia itself had done to increase its Intellectual Capital. The result was a six-step road map to IC creation:

IC PHASES

- Missionary

- Measurement

- Leadership

- IT

- Capitalizing

- Futurizing

1. *Missionary.* This first phase encompasses the initial insights behind an organization recognizing the need to bring to the surface its Intellectual Capital. Typically this begins with a few individual pioneers who identify the underlying problem and convince the rest of the organization of the need for a new perspective. The tools at this level include visualizing metaphors (such as the tree image) as well as the precedent of simple metrics for comparative conversation.

2. *Measurement.* The second phase targets the development of the balancing metrics, the taxonomy, for this new model. Also included is the development of the IC controller function and the initial work in aligning IC measurement with the organization's current accounting system.

3. *Leadership.* Next comes the decision at various levels of the firm to act upon the new insights that arrive from the balanced report perspective. In particular, what is required is a shift from the management of the past to the navigation into the future in terms of renewal and development.

4. *Technology.* This phase emphasizes the development of technology to increase both the "transparency" (that is, ease of seeing) and the packaging of knowledge, as well as the communications systems needed to share that knowledge. At Skandia, the evolution of technology and IC can be traced from Administrative Technology (AT) using mainframes to Information Technology (IT) using PCs to Communications Technologies (CT) on the Internet, to finally, in the case of packaging the IC Annual Report on CD-ROM, Entertainment Technologies (ET).

5. *Capitalizing.* This captures the use of packaged organizational technology (database management systems, sales force automation tools, and the like) as well as intellectual property in the creation of Intellectual Capital. Capitalization is critical to recycling the enterprise's critical knowledge and structural capital investment.

6. *Futurizing.* The last step is the systematic nurturing of innovation as a core competence in the organization to maintain continuous renewal and development, and being on the edge.

It took five years for Skandia to cover these six steps, culminating in 1996 with the creation of the first of the company's Future Centers, which represent a visible commitment to the final, futurizing step "by turning the future into an asset," said Wolrath, "not a liability to future generations." However, it should also be noted that, as sequential and logical as this may now appear, in the messy world of real-life business it mostly occurred in parallel loops, with numerous restarts and unexpected thresholds.

NAVIGATING NEW WATERS

We mentioned earlier that the IC team, with approval of Skandia management, chose to try and create a model that targeted both valuation *and* navigation.

First, valuation. This required a scheme, one that distinguishes the different building blocks that make up Intellectual Capital. As we have seen, the Skandia IC team constructed this scheme by the process of reduction. It began with the stock market valuation of the company, subtracted its financial capital, and what was left as the balancing item was the company's Intellectual Capital. The process continued from there.

Take Intellectual Capital and subtract from it one of the two building blocks, human capital, and the result, as we know from our core equation, is structural capital. Reduce structural capital by customer capital and you are left with organizational capital as the balancing value. Next, from within organizational capital one can subtract the value of processes to leave innovation capital; and then from innovation capital subtract the value of intellectual properties such as patents and trademarks. The final remainder, reduced to a tiny fraction of its traditional scope, would be intangible (that is, undefinable or unmeasurable) assets.

This simplified value scheme can of course be refined and elaborated. But even as it is it offers a format by which indices can be established that best capture the value of each of the components, as well as offers some clues to creating comparisons, ratios, and "dialogues," if you will, between different groups. For example, one could devise a ratio between intellectual property and intangible assets, showing the comparative importance to the organization between what it legally controls and what it has no real control of at all.

Another interesting ratio of this type is between human capital and structural capital—with organizations that undergo this exercise often surprised to discover the former is quite small compared to the latter. This unexpected result suggests the need for leadership to look more closely at its structural capital and its role in creating stakeholder value. Is there a lot of idle, untapped potential within the boundaries of their structural capital? Were this situation to occur in physical capital (say, a truck used only 50 percent of the time), it would attract the immediate attention of leadership and management. But, as structural capital is largely invisible in traditional accounting, this waste is usually ignored.

One goal of the valuation process, then, is to highlight unusual ratio combinations and then test them to see if they yield an unexpected and useful new perspective on the organization. As Gary Hamel of the London School of Economics has said, "Perspective is worth 50 IQ points."

Navigation is a different matter altogether. It can be seen as the search for another language of dynamic reporting beyond management. In particular, it aims to highlight the continuing process of adding to the long-term sustainability of the organization and nurturing the organization's roots for sustainable cash-flow generation.

Ironically, this is where that abandoned one-page IC report of 1993 found a new life—because from it emerged the so-called

Skandia Navigator, which will be described in greater depth in the next chapter. For now, what is important to know is that it emerged out of a matrix of needs, including the desire to tie together all six IC focus areas, show how they interact, and place them in the timescape of the corporation's operating life. Thus, the renewal and development focus relates to the future of the organization, the structural focus to the present, and the financial focus to the immediate past.

The Navigator cleverly linked all of the focuses together into a coherent shape that managed to tell the story of IC's role in the organization. A person coming to the Navigator for the first time could, after a few minutes, understand the component parts of a company's Intellectual Capital assets, how they worked together, and what role they played in the corporation's activities. Not bad for a few colored squares and triangles.

The Navigator played another role as well—that of serving as a table of contents for mapping the organization's IC patterns. Like chapters in a book, the different focuses defined the territory of each cluster of measurements. The organization could then articulate a business concept for its future, as well as its core mission and goals. These strategies were then translated into critical success factors, and those in turn were transformed into metrics. Finally the metrics themselves were sorted into five focus areas and used either to winnow through existing indicators or develop new ones. Thus, the Skandia Navigator first served its designers as a developmental tool, then, in its first public appearance in 1995's *Visualizing Intellectual Capital,* it took on a new role as an organizer and guide to users.

IC MANAGEMENT

Before it is a tool for investors and analysts, the Navigator and the indicators it contains are first and foremost an aid to the company's leadership.

If there is one thing the Navigator makes abundantly clear it is that the management of Intellectual Capital is more than just knowledge or intellectual property management. IC management is in fact the leveraging of human capital and structural capital in combination.[4]

INTELLECTUAL CAPITAL MANAGEMENT

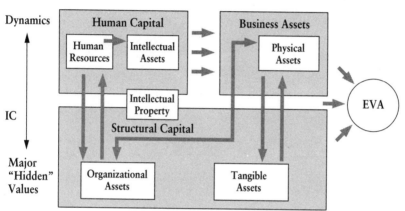

From this one can derive that effective IC management is the result of a four-step process:

1. Understand those parts of the Navigator that show the capability for value creation and value extraction.
2. Leverage this value by the interaction and cross-fertilization of idle capabilities.
3. Focus on the flow and exchange, the "transparency," of competencies in the organization by creating a buffet of knowledge (Skandia not surprisingly called it a "smorgasbord") from which stakeholders can pick out what they need to be more productive.
4. Capitalize on this process by releasing, codifying, recycling, and exchanging its components.

The benefits of this process are both deep and wide. They include:

- A steeper learning curve.
- Shortened lead time to application.
- Savings in cost and investment on structural capital and organizational capital, some of it through recycling.
- Greater added value through improved interactions.
- New value creation by novel connections and combinations.

But of course all of this is meaningless unless, as was the case at Skandia, management is committed to the IC development and measurement process and to using this information to rethink the company's organization, its strengths and weaknesses, and its future.

STAKING OUT THE FUTURE

That brings us nearly to the present in the Skandia IC story. Having taken a compelling new idea—that intangible corporate assets could be defined, measured, and put to use to improve company competitiveness and attractiveness—Skandia pioneered a new field by developing an underlying philosophy, a body of metrics and indicators, and even an organizing tool.

With the 1995 supplement and its successors, Skandia has chosen, at least for now, not to aggregate the data from individual company units into an overall corporate report. Rather, the company has decided to continue to develop its reporting expertise and to further refine the Navigator as both a planning tool and a follow-up tool.

Most recently, Skandia has begun to experiment with using the Navigator for individual performance appraisal and assessment. The goal is to devise a balanced reward system that contains both financial as well as nonfinancial dimensions. Already this program has produced a possible new employee incentive and reward instrument, an IC "option," that may well prove the commodity of exchange in some future IC stock market (see chapter 12).

A final innovation from Skandia. It is the company's attempt to answer the question: Once you understand your company's Intellectual Capital, what do you do with that insight?

One answer is that you've got to share it not only throughout the organization but with strategic partners, even customers. And that requires using the newest and best information and communications technology to enrich the message and speed up its delivery.

Another answer is that you apply that knowledge right at the edge between human capital and renewal and development, as well as at the junction between the company's internal organization and its operating environment—and use it to foster innovation as the very purpose of sustained enterprise. Why? Because, in Peter Drucker's memorable words, "Every organization—not just business—needs one core competence: innovation. And every organization needs a way to record and appraise its innovative performance." IC, for the first time, makes that possible, and it would be foolish not to do so.

It was to achieve both of these goals that, in 1996, Skandia opened its first Skandia Future Center (SFC) at Villa Askudden in Waxholm, on the Swedish archipelago north of Stockholm. This center, the first of several planned throughout the world, is chartered to leverage Skandia's, as well as external specialists', collective intelligence by systematically developing and sharing knowledge, creating new applications and competencies, and establishing communications systems for their dissemination throughout the organization.

As Skandia itself defined the role of these centers, they are to be:

- A strategic concept to turn the future into an asset, not a liability,

61

- A process of collective intelligence and collaboration across generations, cultures, and functions (known as the "3G [Generations] Approach"), and
- A networked virtual organization, combining internal as well as external knowledge sources.

In particular, the SFCs are assigned to increase Skandia's strategic readiness as well as its rapidness to turn the future into an asset. That can only be done if the centers continuously scan for and identify new challenges, options, and industry dynamics the instant they appear. Then they must create new navigational, processing, and leveraging tools to capture and use those potential new advantages.

That's a tall order, but one for which Skandia is right now better prepared than almost any company on the planet, thanks to its pioneering work in Intellectual Capital and its commitment to innovation.

THE FUTURE OF THE FUTURE

Skandia's innovation culture has been described as a wave that is kept in constant motion by the flow of ideas and competencies with it. Yet at the same time, it can also be seen as a gradual evolution, beginning with a division between human and service assets; to viewing projects, companies, clients, and even knowledge as assets; to ultimately seeing the future itself as an asset—and thereby leveraging into a second, third, or higher life cycle curve.

This last evolutionary step, called *futurization,* operates in the border zone between human capital and structural capital, because after all, success comes not just from new ideas but from their implementation—and that implementation is the product of the corporate culture, leadership, and supportive infrastructure.

Companies that can identify the driving forces in their operating environment at an early stage and can divert them to create new business opportunities—while at the same time refining existing operations—will be tomorrow's winners. They will have futurized themselves, turning the future into an asset by the power of innovation.

By paving the path this far, Skandia has given other companies and organizations a gift of Intellectual Capital. They can vault over the preliminary steps and take their own IC measurement system right up into the present. The intention of the rest of this book is to push the process even further into new applications.

And that's where we go from here. First, a tour of the Navigator and all its component parts. Then off to take Intellectual Capital into unexplored territory.

◆ 4 ◆

Navigating Through a New World

The more complex a business environment, the more sophisticated the tools we need to operate in it. Yet, at the same time, if that tool is to be of universal use, it also must be simple to operate.

Not an easy task. Traditional accounting is essentially a one-dimensional process: Columns of raw data are summed and then inserted into a dual-column format—the balance sheet—according to specific rules—algorithms—of organization. In this respect, it is a *presentational* tool.

To scrutinize this format, you simply run down each column, translating the numbers back according to the file in which they have been placed. Thus, you know when you read under "accounts payable" the figure $1,325 that the company still owes that amount to its suppliers. By comparing this number to others in that statement or in other companies' statements, you can then draw your own conclusions ("They're deadbeats and not paying their bills" or "They're brilliantly stringing out their payables to make money on the money").

The traditional balance sheet also plays a secondary (some investors might even say primary) role as a *navigational* tool. It does this almost in spite of itself: As you read through the columns of figures you encounter symbols for footnotes, important information that literally lies off the page. As any stock analyst will tell you, within these footnotes and other accompanying documentation often can be found the real soul of the enterprise.

It may have lost a key manager, or the CEO is being sued by a former employee for sexual harassment, or the company is being granted a major operating license for a potentially big new market. Or it may be that the company has just been awarded the patent on the most important new invention in a generation. The possibilities are as broad as human nature.

These entries are also often maddeningly obscure, precisely because the company writing them does not want to make this disclosure and the rules of accounting allow them considerable latitude. That's why analysts often spend hours trying to decode them, as if they were archaeologists studying Babylonian tablets.

You may also realize by now that these footnotes are often as close as the traditional accounting system comes to actually addressing the question of Intellectual Capital—which is why these pages of tight text are considered so valuable.

In fact, from one perspective, it might be said that the study of Intellectual Capital is in fact the search for ways to systematically capture, elucidate, and leverage the subjective, half-hidden information about a company now hidden in footnotes to its balance sheet.

In the words of Dorothy Leonard-Barton of the Harvard Business School, speaking to *Industry Week:*

> Knowledge accumulates slowly, over time, shaped and channeled into certain directions through the nudging of hundreds of daily managerial decisions. Nor does knowledge occur only one time; it is constantly aborning. . . . Knowledge reservoirs in organizations are not static pools but wellsprings, constantly replenished with streams of new ideas and constituting an ever-flowing source of corporate renewal.[1]

How can one create an intellectual radar to identify and measure such an elusive target? The first step is to recognize that no one-dimensional format is going to work for such disparate types of information. The second step is to appreciate that whereas traditional accounting is, by design, primarily a presentational tool of the past, Intellectual Capital is, by default, primarily a navigational tool of the future. By default, we mean that it takes on as its governance the vast territories of data that lie beyond the small, enclosed compound directed by traditional accounting. Says Karl-Erik Sveiby, "In order to 'see' the knowledge organization, try to regard your organization as if it consists of knowledge structures, rather than [financial] capital."[2]

As described in chapter 2, Intellectual Capital might be viewed as two forms: human and structural (three, if you separate out customer capital). This alone should tell us that any navigational tool we develop will have to be at least two- dimensional. No simple one-to-one comparing of one number to another is going to work with both indicators and indices this different. Rather, we can assume that these different types of capital will have distinct *regions* of influence, and that there may be other freestanding regions as well. Within each of these regions will lie the metrics that best describe them.

Somehow, then, all of these regions must be pulled together into an overall format, a taxonomy, that not only displays all of this information but provides the outside viewer with a quick and obvious way to enter the presentation and easily navigate in and among these different regions. To draw a comparison with a more traditional form of navigation, what is needed in Intellectual Capital is a map that captures all of the value of an enterprise, color-coded so that one can quickly ascertain the quality of the topology—where there are swamps and lush forests, mountains and deserts.

THE SKANDIA IC NAVIGATOR

To date, Skandia has been the only company to construct such a tool, which it properly calls the Skandia Navigator. It looks like this:

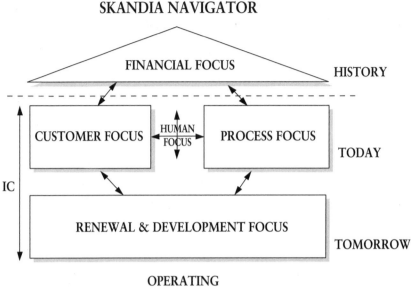

SKANDIA NAVIGATOR

Though constantly being modified, the Skandia Navigator has already proven to be so effective that it will likely be the basis for most future IC navigation tools.

First, notice its organization. It is composed not of types of capital but of five areas of *focus*. In other words, these are the areas upon which an enterprise focuses its attention, and from that focus comes the value of the company's Intellectual Capital within its competitive environment.

Now, note the shape of the Navigator. It is essentially a house, Skandia's visual metaphor for the organization itself. The triangle atop the rectangle, the attic one could say, is the **Financial Focus,** which includes our old friend the balance sheet. The Financial Focus is the past of the firm, a precise measure of where it was at a specific moment. The indicators of this focus are for the most part well established; however, the notion of "focus" allows for the addition of new measures, notably ratios suggesting performance, speed, and quality, as well.

Now, as we move down the form, to the walls of the house of

Intellectual Capital, we enter the present and the company activities that focus upon it. These are **Customer Focus** and **Process Focus**, the first measuring a distinct type of Intellectual Capital, the second part of the larger measure of structural capital.

Finally, the bottom of the IC rectangle, the foundation of our house, looks at the future. This is the **Renewal & Development Focus**, the other part of structural capital. The indices in this region measure not only how well the company is preparing itself for the future through employee training, new product development, and the like but how effectively it is abandoning the obsolete past through product turnover, abandonment of dwindling markets, and other strategic actions. It also addresses the likely business environment in which the organization will operate.

There is one last focus we haven't yet addressed. It lies at the center of the house, as well it should, since it is the heart, the intelligence, and the soul of the organization. Moreover, as the only active force in the organization, it touches all of the other IC regions. This is the **Human Focus**, the first half of the overall IC model. This is the part of the company that goes home every night. And it consists of the competence and capabilities of employees, the commitment by the company to help keep those skills regularly tuned and updated and to support them with outside experts. Finally, it is the mix of experience and innovation found in these employees and the company's strategies for changing or maintaining this mix.

NAVIGATIONAL TASKS

That is the structure of the Navigator. But we have not yet spoken of the goals of this tool and its coming counterparts.

An effective IC Navigator must efficiently fulfill three tasks:

1. *Look down into the measurements.* An organizing tool fails in its duty if it does not organize. That goes without

saying. But the best tools must do more than that; they must act as a guide—that is, as a navigator, rather than merely a file cabinet—to the right body of measurements, link them together in a coherent way by category, then tie all of those categories together into a cohesive whole. It must show the position, direction, and velocity of the organization. As we'll see in the next section, it is important that any contemporary Navigator be organized in such a way as to take full advantage of the presentational technologies of the future.

2. *Look upward toward more sweeping measures of value.* It is not enough that a navigational tool serve as a headliner and a tour guide. It must also function in such a way as to process all of this data into a higher order of abstraction to get a perspective. That is, a good IC Navigator must ultimately align all of the categorical data for the creation of just a handful of overall figures—"metaindices," one might call them, comparable to profit and loss on a income statement, or total assets and total liabilities on a balance sheet—that can be used for a quick thumbnail judgment of a company's IC strength and for comparison with other organizations.

3. *Look outward toward the user.* This may seem self-evident as well. But comprehensibility and inclusiveness are a lot easier in theory than they are in practice. Even for millions of businesspeople, the modern financial accounting system is hopelessly obscure, the entries ("allowance for uncollectibles") neither intuitive nor, once you learn the definition, especially precise. Neither, as we have seen, does the balance sheet fully encompass all of the value-creating activities of the enterprise—the rest of them are either unrecognized or buried in the verbiage of the accompanying footnotes.

This is not to disparage traditional accounting. It has been the most powerful tool in the bookkeeping arsenal for centuries.

Moreover, it has been studied, revised, and encoded by thousands of academics over generations of study. Rather, the lesson is this: To blithely assume that any new measurement model will, right out of the gate, escape obscurantism while still capturing all of the useful information we desire is both arrogant and naive. It will take years to perfect both the model of Intellectual Capital and the tools needed to present it.

The good news is that with the Navigator, the product of thousands of hours of exploration by a multidisciplined team, Skandia has already taken the rest of us a good ways down that road. Is Skandia's IC Navigator the perfect tool for the job? Does it fulfill our three roles?

Not quite. But it is a good start. Time and necessity should do the rest.

A NEW VALUE DIMENSION

Double-entry bookkeeping was a product of the late Medieval collision of Arabic symbolic mathematics and European paper-making. Modern accounting lies at the nexus of communications, high-speed/low-cost printing, and very fast computational tools.

The reporting of Intellectual Capital has evolved from the late stages of this previous era, but moves beyond it. The rise of IC can been seen as a product of the information era:[3] When you empower individual employees through the use of computers, the Internet, and high-speed digital telecommunications, the organization becomes so agile, quick, and adaptive—so *organic*—in its behavior that traditional static tools for measuring value quickly become hopelessly anachronistic.

If IC reporting is to cover this new business reality, it stands to reason that it must also manifest that reality. As presently configured, the IC Annual Report still bears the stamp of an older time. Even its title suggests the problem: annual. In its current form, such a report can provide the shape of a company's Intellectual Capital, but only part of its dynamic.

The missing element is *time*. We need to add a third dimension to the current two: one that shows the changing values in real time, like the gauges on an automobile dashboard.[4] Best of all, we need to show those indicators being continuously modified by other, related, indicators or indices. Thus, total sales might be modified on one display by total transactions per hour, on another by customer satisfaction, and another by closed versus lost contracts.

The result would be the Navigator moving through time, always up-to-the-minute, but also leaving a trail of all of the past minutes to show improvement or decline. Like a person attached to a patient-monitoring system, such an IC measurement process would quickly detect corporate excitement, exhaustion, stress, weakness, and illness. This would be a truly dynamic reporting of Intellectual Capital.

And we can go one step further. Today, when we value a company through the price of its stock, that stock's price fluctuates not only with sales and earnings but with new product introductions and the response those announcements have upon industry opinion makers. It also is affected by the hiring or firing of key employees, and by the public statements and predictions of senior management. Baruch Lev has suggested that as much as 95 percent of a stock's price variation is related to nonfinancial information.[5]

In the best of all scenarios, our IC Navigator would not only move forward in time, but it would also step off the page, capture this huge body of relevant information with not only figures and ratios but also multimedia product presentations (with comments from reviewers), videos and transcripts of executive speeches, interviews and résumés of senior managers, a video tour of key facilities, and the like. Further, viewers, both professional analysts and private investors, would be able to tour these files and clips, perhaps in time (through virtual reality) walk the floors of the manufacturing plant or take the product for a test run.

Most of this is available right now, via high-speed modem lines, advanced displays, sales force automation databases, and Internet Web sites. The rest will be along soon enough, most likely long before consensus on a common Navigator or its contents are reached. All that is needed is the will and commitment to make it real. And is there any doubt that the company that does so first in its field will draw the greatest attention of analysts and investors? Or that its commitment to accurate and complete disclosure will be rewarded for its own merit? By the same token, does any reader believe that once the average investor sees this new reporting model that he or she will demand it from every company as a precondition to investment?

Three-D IC is still ahead of us. For now, the immediate—and greater—challenge is to understand Intellectual Capital and agree upon how to measure and present it. That will be the subject of the next four chapters, as we look at each of the IC factors and their indices in turn.

Real Value: The Financial Focus

We begin with the traditional start: finance.

The movement of money through an organization is, ulti-mately, the most tangible measure of its value. It is also the source of its rewards in terms of profits, salaries, and earnings. That's why money has been the centerpiece of company record keeping at least since the Sumerians.

The history of business, beneath all of the changes in technol-ogy, organization, and management theory, is really just the story of how to attach monetary value to activity and assets. That is, in fact, what is occurring with the rise of Intellectual Capital—with the added recognition that new activities and assets have appeared and that either their true value, as translated to money, may take a much longer time than comparable factors in the past, or, conversely, they are so dynamic as to radically change the value of the organization too quickly for the traditional financial reporting cycle.

So far this book has put on a sidetrack the financial pages of an annual report, suggesting that the balance sheet, earnings statement, supporting footnotes, and other documents are essen-tially a hermetic document, useful in its own right as a snapshot of where the enterprise has been as it has manifested its achieve-ments as cash, equipment, and plant. However, at the same time there has been the implicit suggestion that the financial state-ment is actually a subset of the larger IC report, capturing, as it were, one component of a much larger analysis of a company's worth.

Obviously, this creates something of a paradox. The financials can't be independent of the IC report yet still part of it. So the questions become:

- How do traditional financials relate to the larger measurement of Intellectual Capital?
- How are these traditional financial documents changed by their relation to the new measurement of Intellectual Capital?
- What represents sustainable earnings potential?

In the world of Intellectual Capital, the financials take on the new role of *repository.* The process may take decades or hours, but at some point in the future, all Intellectual Capital, if it is to have value, must convert to currency (or some, as yet undefined, substitute). A new technology may take months to develop and years to convert to a real product, but at some point it must turn into revenues for the enterprise. By the same token, indices of customer satisfaction, employee morale, and the like must also manifest themselves as higher revenues, lower overhead, or greater profits—or just the opposite. As that conversion occurs, that measure moves up from renewal and development, to customer and process, to at last an entry in the financials—and thence, into the company's financial history.

But it works the other way as well. The financials offer the best feedback system for testing the effectiveness of the focuses. In particular, if a certain index or indicator *never* makes itself felt on the balance sheet, then it actually measures nothing of value and should be purged. As Intellectual Capital develops and its measures and forms become standardized, the financial test will play a crucial role in establishing those standards.

Recognizing this symbiotic relationship, it is obvious that, embedded as they are within an Intellectual Capital report, the financial pages cannot themselves be inviolate. More than being just a repository for feedback information, they also must over time change to better fit the other focuses. In the near term, this will probably not entail a revamping of current accounting standards—that would be both too much of a shock to the financial system and certainly premature given than none of these metrics are fully proven in widespread use.

Instead, the process will certainly be more organic, the result of trial and error. New measures of value should migrate onto the balance sheet, while older, now anachronistic entries (say, the value of land at its purchase price) should migrate off. Still others (such as stock options) should remain but change their definition or metric. This will happen, however, only if passageways—both structural and procedural—are put in place to allow these migrations to occur. The structural channels, as we will now show, are provided by the new Intellectual Capital model. The procedural passageways (or knowing human nature, perhaps it is more accurate to say, the procedural *gates* on the structural channels) will be opened only by a change in the mind-set of current ruling bodies. The record of FASB with stock options suggests this may prove the most difficult of all.

But if this free circulation can be instituted, it will result in a kind of continuous upwelling of new indices and sinking of archaic ones within the structure of financial capital. To see how this would work, take our triangle "roof" that represents the Financial Focus and further divide it as shown on page 78.

RAW FINANCIAL DATA

At the base of Financial Focus triangle are the subjective, nonempirical, and undifferentiated financial notes of the enterprise. This section encompasses what is currently found in financial notes of the company's annual report, press releases announcing major new contracts, divisional performance evaluations, analyst evalu-

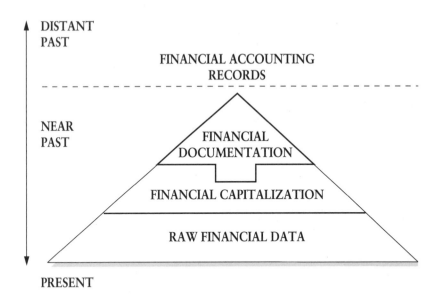

DISTANT PAST

FINANCIAL ACCOUNTING RECORDS

NEAR PAST

FINANCIAL DOCUMENTATION

FINANCIAL CAPITALIZATION

RAW FINANCIAL DATA

PRESENT

ations, and so forth. It can be seen as being fresh financial news just emerging from the customer, human, and process operations of the company. Much of this material is very valuable, some of it may profoundly impact the company's book value. But as yet it has not been refined to the point where it can be measured and evaluated according to any accepted metric.

Perceiving this information this way has several advantages. For one thing, it recognizes that the footnotes and other subjective documents of traditional financial reporting merely reflect the inability of those documents to accurately capture all of the information vital to evaluating a company. Putting them now below a new evaluation process shows they no longer carry the same reporting responsibility . . . and meanwhile puts the onus of capturing the truths in those notes upon the new measurement system. Another way of looking at it is that any footnote or side document that now appears with a balance sheet can be judged a failure of the Intellectual Capital model that must be addressed.

Second, this new format also recognizes that, in the newly wired enterprise, relevant financial data is now embedded in every operation of the company. Modern corporate accounting is no longer a distinct and independent operation within the company whose task is to add up receipts and cut checks and compute profits at the end of the quarter. Rather, it is now indistinguishable from the rest of the enterprise network. The modern organization is a place where financial data, gathered by the minute, races around from database to database within the organization; where a new asset is created this morning by a clever salesperson or lost this afternoon by a lazy corporate bureaucrat; and most of all, where success or failure for an entire company may rest upon a tactical decision made by a senior executive based upon full corporate financial data that must be up-to-date to that very moment.

Thus, the simple title "Raw Financials" actually encompasses something close to chaos. It may mean trillions of bits of data, rumors, verbal promises, reports from field salespeople, patent attorneys, appraisers, and scores of other blocks of financial information. Some of it is worthless, some of it dangerously misguided, and some of it not worth the time needed to pursue it in greater depth. On the other hand, some of this data may be useful and of enduring value, or it may be useful but evanescent. And it may be of wide application or of limited utility.

In the deluge of data streaming into the corporate offices, a wave that grows higher and stronger every year, no company has the time or resources to explore every drop. Nor is it fair, as we do today, to reduce all this information to a few purposefully obscure (but within the law) paragraphs of notes in the annual report and to innuendo and gossip that automatically confers a huge investment edge to corporate insiders.

The only solution is to find those measures that will hack through this information undergrowth, find the promising sites, then filter out the worthless gravel and sand to leave the gold nuggets we are searching for.

FINANCIAL CAPITALIZATION

The process of searching and filtering, of translating and measuring, this raw information occurs in the center of the triangle, in Financial Capitalization. Here is where the new IC metrics appear. They are, in a sense, a new and more sophisticated type of pattern recognition demanded by the changing business environment. These metrics are designed to produce indices and indicators that separate the gold of the undifferentiated information from the dross of superfluous data, generalizations, opinion, and spurious results. The measures of Financial Capitalization, the major contribution of the IC model to traditional finance, are of great importance to the enterprise—but as their location suggests, their contribution is more as a barometer to the current operation of the firm than as a reference to the company's financial archives.

One cannot stress enough how well-considered these Financial Capital measures must be. They must be both penetrating in their ability to capture the truly valuable assets of the enterprise, while at the same time be sufficiently inclusive to capture *all* of those assets.

Needless to say, a huge challenge . . . and one that will never be fully achieved. Nevertheless, anything is better than the obtuse addenda we are forced to live with now. Anything, however, is not enough. What is needed is an initial collection of indices and indicators that is sufficient in precision and scope to set a baseline standard that can amended with time and experience.

Skandia, when it set out to develop its first public IC annual report, scrutinized the financial activities of its divisions and reported twenty financial indicators. They are as follows (unit of measurement is noted):

1. *Fund assets ($).* Keep in mind that Skandia is a financial services firm, and thus many of its indices, such as this one, relate to that industry. However, it is easy to map most of

these indices over into manufacturing, services, and as we'll see later, nonprofit institutions and government.

2. *Fund assets/employee ($)*. Note that in this index and the next we are entering into an area that is well off the balance sheet and only occasionally appears elsewhere in an annual report. This is the actual performance of the individual employee—contribution to the company, span of control, leverage of skills, customer service, and the like. These quotients are a standard part of business, performed by managers and analysts, but until now they have not received much formal attention—yet it is employee productivity that is often the true measure of a company's long-term chances of success.

3. *Income/employee ($)*.

4. *Income/managed assets (%)*.

5. *Premium income ($)*.

6. *Premium income resulting from a new business operation ($)*. Here is a measure not just of revenues but also of regeneration: How well are the company's new businesses performing? This, combined with indicators from other focuses dealing with new product development and employee training, offers a glimpse into how the company is likely to perform in the years to come.

7. *Invoicing/employee ($)*.

8. *Customer time/employee attendance (%)*. This measure is to be distinguished from the increasingly popular ancillary indicator used by many companies of "customer time (or invoicing)/revenue person." The Skandia indicator counts all employees, including administrative personnel, managers, accounting staff, and human resources staff. Thus it is a much truer measure of the company's commitment to customer-related activities. It is also interesting to note that after Skandia saw this ratio (which was 72 percent for the one division measured in 1994), it then set a goal of 74 percent for the following year. This suggests yet one

more role for IC indices beyond serving as the on-deck circle for the financial pages; and that is as an immediate feedback device for spotting vulnerabilities and strengths as well as setting near-term structural performance goals.

9. *Insurance result/employee ($).*
10. *Loss ratio compared to market average (%).* This deals with Skandia's aviation insurance business unit, but it suggests a larger theme, that of an industrywide comparison to create a ratio or an index of customer loyalty.
11. *Direct yield (%).*
12. *Net operating income ($).*
13. *Market value ($).*
14. *Market value/employee ($).*
15. *Return on net asset value (%).*
16. *Return on net assets resulting from a new business operation ($).*
17. *Value added/employee ($).* In Skandia's experience, this is the most important indicator of this group, as it is the least distorted by "creative" accounting.
18. *IT expense/administrative expense (%).*
19. *Value added/IT-employees ($).* Note that this entry essentially combines the two that precede it, creating a multidimensional, multivariable image of how the employees and the information technology of the firm work together to add value to the firm.
20. *Investments in IT ($).*

From Skandia's list one can detect a pattern of four different types of indices:

1. *Cumulative.* A direct measure, usually in monetary terms, of some finance-related business activity, for example, "market value." Cumulative measures are often useful for spotting points of inflection—turning points—in life cycle curves.

2. *Competitive.* A measure, typically as a percentage or index, that compares some part of the company's performance to that of its industry, for example, "loss ratio compared to market average." Competitive measures are typically the source of benchmarks.

3. *Comparative.* A ratio that includes two company-based variables, for example, "value added per employee." Comparative ratios are usually the best source of information about company dynamics.

4. *Combined.* A hybrid quotient, expressed either in monetary terms or as a ratio, that combines more than two company-based variables, for example, "return on net assets resulting from a new business expense." Combined ratios are often used to provide unexpected new perspectives on an organization.

In their upcoming book *IC Visualizing and Measuring,*[1] Johan and Goran Roos go one step further. They argue that any such measures, to be useful and accurate for outside observers *and* practical to those inside the company facing the quotidian task of doing the measurements, must exhibit four inherent characteristics. They must be:

1. Relevant
2. Precise
3. Dimensionless (that is, sweeping in scope)
4. Easy to measure

(We'll revisit the Roos requirements later in the book when we create our universal indicators.)

It is interesting to note that whereas traditional accounting is weighted toward the cumulative indicators, it is the other three indices that hold the most immediate value to an executive. It can even be suggested that within this middle ground of Financial

Capital there is also an ascending order going from immediate usefulness to translation onto the balance sheet.

In other words, the more complex, far-reaching and multivariable the index, the more likely it is to capture information of immediate use by the company in its daily activities. Then, with time, this combined index matures into a comparative index that can be used to compare performance with the competition, then further stabilizes into a cumulative measure indicator as it prepares for the jump to the balance sheet. Interestingly, as we will see, this hierarchy is turned upside down with Intellectual Capital reporting.

Obviously that is simplistic, but it does offer a philosophical underpinning to creation of financial capital metrics. It suggests that what is needed is a balanced mix between the four index types, though the combined indices may be much more difficult to gather than the cumulative indicators. Moreover it also suggests that although all decision makers in the company need all of this information, line managers ought to put more emphasis on the more immediate, combined measurements, while staff should look to the competitive and cumulative data. This, of course, is precisely what business gurus like Michael Hammer and Rosabeth Moss Kanter have been saying for a long time. Now we have not only empirical validation of their ideas but a systematic way of getting that information.

So what does the reader do with this information? Well, if you happen to be in the financial services industry, you are in luck: Skandia has already found a core group of measurements for you to use and build upon. The bad news is that Skandia's already been doing these measurements—and learning greatly from them—for several years. You'd better get moving.

For everybody else, in manufacturing or a different service industry, the bad news is that you have to start from scratch. On the other hand, as nobody else has done it either (though that will probably change very soon), you've got a leg up on the competition and a chance to gain a competitive edge.

In the meantime, to give you a running start, consider these possible indices for your own company and industry, some of them derived from Skandia's list, some of them new:

1. Total assets ($)
2. Total assets/employee ($)
3. Revenues/total assets (%)
4. Profits/total assets ($)
5. Revenues resulting from new business operations ($)
6. Profits resulting from a new business operations ($)
7. Revenues/employee ($)
8. Customer time/employee attendance (%)
9. Profits/employee ($)
10. Lost business revenues compared to market average (%)
11. Revenues from new customers/total revenues (%)
12. Market value ($)
13. Market value/employee ($)
14. Return on net asset value (%)
15. Return on net assets resulting from a new business operation ($)
16. Value added/employee ($)
17. IT expense/administrative expense (%)
18. Value added/IT-employees ($)
19. Investments in IT ($)
20. Value added/customer
21. R&D investment

FINANCIAL DOCUMENTATION

Finally, at the apex of the triangle, the "main beam," stand the traditional financial tables. They represent the final transmutation of individual Intellectual Capital assets into cash value—and thus their disappearance from the daily life of the firm and from our "house." Here, after the raw financial material has been gathered, then processed through the Financial Capital metrics, formalized data is ready to be presented in final, permanent form. Here the documents stand as a monument to the company's success or failure at converting its Intellectual Capital into financial value—at least until the end of the current measurement cycle, when they are replaced by a successive accounting.

These annual financial tables, in leaving the "near past" of the firm, enter a larger triangle than the one we have been describing. This is the accumulated financial documentation of the company since the day it was founded—from the check written to file the original articles of incorporation to yesterday's reams of paychecks, bills, receipts, bank drafts, and so forth. This vast pyramid, whose base grows wider by the year as the company grows and the archives pile higher, also includes quarterly and yearly earnings statements, balance sheets, tax forms, and audit data.

In the future it may also include Intellectual Capital information. Certainly it will do so if the company, like Skandia, prepares an IC Annual Report. But more interesting is whether those archives will include IC data that is *integrated* with the financial documents of the firm. In other words, will there be some financial IC data that is considered so valuable that it endures in the company's records as a permanent addition to the traditional accounting documents?

The question is interesting, because, as we noted earlier, some of the financial Intellectual Capital indices being proposed may very well migrate onto the balance sheet in years to come. Thus, what we are really seeing is three distinct forces at work in the assimilation of Intellectual Capital to the financial operations of a company:

1. The *push* from inside the company to identify the heretofore unknown or unappreciated forces that create value and to spot idle soft assets.
2. The *pull* of company executives, investors, and strategic

partners for information on the company's strengths and vulnerabilities, and how it is preparing itself for the future.

3. The *deep pull* from the company's past to identify those factors that have made it a success (or failure), to learn deeply from its mistakes, to capture and preserve any information that might be of competitive use by the company in the future, and to identify opportunity points in the company's life cycle curve. To this deep pull we think you can add one more force driving IC onto the balance sheet:

4. The *deep push* from what we already anticipate about the changed nature of the future to find new perspectives on how the business works, new measures of what value is, and new notions of what constitutes success.[2]

Nowhere are all of these forces more at play than in the definition of profit. And it seems likely that the most likely place where IC indices will appear and stay on the balance sheet and earnings statement is in modifying the presentation of that always controversial topic.

Profit is a notoriously elusive measurement. The biggest reason is that profit is generally perceived as the ne plus ultra index of a company's short-term success. Thus, it is the target of politicians, tax collectors, union negotiators, and managers trying to pump the company up or hold down investor expectations. Profits are borrowed from the future or deferred to it, minimized by intentional losses or write-offs, or inflated for near-term gain by sacrificing the company's future.

Once again, professional investors know this and, with the right market intelligence, usually know when to account for such tactics; but average investors do not. For that reason, it is easy to imagine certain combined and comparative financial IC measurements being used to break up traditional profit/loss entries on the financial pages into small and more useful subcategories.

For example, breaking down net profits into those contributed by products less than two years old and those by products greater than two years old would help answer the deep push from the future for information on whether the company is coasting on past successes or preparing itself for the years to come. Meanwhile, a breakdown of gross profit margins by the middle six months of the fiscal year compared to the bracketing six months might answer the deep pull of the company's historical archives for a measure of how much the company is pumping itself up (or leaning itself out) by playing with its books on the fringes of the year.

There are scores of other ways that IC information *may* come to modify the balance sheet and earnings statement. But which *will* do so is not something that will be known except at the end of a long process of experimentation, validation, and assimilation. IC measurements will cross over to the financials when it is hard to imagine those documents without that information—and that will come only after investors and managers have worked with IC reports for a long time and begun to think in their unique grammar the way we do accounting entries today. And even then, it will take the approval of the Brahmins that set current accounting standards, a group that is not—and should not—rush to any judgment.

But such policies and procedures should be the least of our concerns right now. The immediate challenge is to begin establishing and refining IC financial metrics, start measuring and reporting them, and then test their usefulness in daily working life. Finally, the results need to be shared with everyone else in industry—because a standard held by one is no standard at all.

That same rule holds for each of the IC focuses that follow. It's time now to get out of the stuffy attic and down into the living part of the house.

Real Worth: The Customer Focus

We are now decades past the once common idea that customers are essentially one-time targets that can be forgotten once the sale is made. Companies that subscribed to that philosophy too long paid dearly for their stubbornness.

Today, if most companies are not quite to the goal of "total customer service," many are certainly straining toward it. And sitting out beyond that is the even more intimidating notion of what Debra M. Amadon calls "customer success," the collaboration with customers in joint value creation.[1]

In the process of trying to reach these goals, companies are applying considerable quantities of corporate resources as well as a wide range of new technological tools to the task of keeping customers satisfied, even ecstatic, for as long as possible.

There are very good reasons for doing this.

New Types of Products and Services

The digital revolution has not only created gigantic new industries, such as personal computing and semiconductors, but those products have in turn transformed in some way almost every product and service in the world.

For example, the performance of appliances, such as washing machines, televisions, and telephones, has been radically transformed by the addition of microprocessors. By adding tiny electronic brains to these systems, the appliances become more adaptive, more flexible but precise in their use, and even upgradeable. The same is true for everything from automobiles and jet aircraft to traffic lights and kitchen stoves. Medical equipment, office supplies, factory equipment, even clothing have also been radically changed by the arrival of low-cost, silicon chip digital intelligence.

If the product itself can't be changed by silicon, then almost always some other part of its creation, delivery, and use can. Thus, programmable robots weld sheet metal, small computerized lens grinders make one-hour eyeglass lenses, and the cappuccino machine at the corner café knows when to stop foaming the milk. Electronic bar code readers and laser checkout scanners automatically adjust inventory, then electronically order replacements.

The service industries as well have been revolutionized by digital intelligence—as anyone knows who has used an ATM machine at midnight, ordered items over the Internet, or caught the last flight home thanks to a quick ticket transfer on an airline reservation computer.

There are currently nearly two hundred million computers in use around the world, six hundred million televisions, and, after just two years of general availability, nearly 100 million users of the Internet. Those are staggering figures, but they pale next to the world's installed base of twelve *billion* microprocessors and microcontrollers. All of these are turning society upside down, not least of which by constantly upping the ante among competitors for how they interact with their customers.[2]

New Types of Customers

Success breeds its own expectations. The consumer of 1960, immersed in a mass-produced society, was accustomed to one-size-fits-all/single-transaction/zero-service relationships with his vendors. The consumer of 1997, having enjoyed a decade of growing control over the purchase process, expects to be able to personally define the product or service to match his or her needs. The modern consumer also expects to be fully trained in the product's use, wants it to never break down—or if it does to have a service rep quickly on-site, on the phone, or on-line—and assumes there will be a smooth software, if not hardware, upgrade path when the next generation of the product appears in a year or so. The same is true for services. The modern consumer wants immediate, customized, flawless delivery, be it from a drive-thru restaurant or a datalog.

Give us customers total satisfaction and we want total success; give us that and we want delight and ecstasy . . . and, presumably, so on to delirium and bliss. And rightly so, because some vendor out there has already found the right combination or personnel and technology to raise the service bar just that much higher to beat the competition. And once we consumers see it can be done (Nordstrom, Motorola, Southwest Airlines), we demand it from everyone.

The result is that companies are increasingly trapped in a race to guarantee the perfect success of their customers—and that creates a whole new set of challenges. Customer satisfaction, we've found, is comparatively easy to achieve: 800 numbers, top-notch quality, quick service and support response, and the like. But once the customer game gets taken to the higher levels, it quickly becomes apparent that no amount of internal corporate resources, used alone, will be enough.

Rather, the customer must tell you what he or she wants to achieve. That may sound easy, but for two little problems:

1. Customers don't necessarily know what they want, especially when it involves a new product, service, or technology they know nothing about. So you must know so much about your customers' tastes, needs, and interests that you can *anticipate* and, with luck, *channel* their demand.

2. But you can only know that much about your customers if

they provide you with stunning amounts of personal information. That requires enormous trust—and how many contemporary companies enjoy such faith by their customers? Not many, and that is why the successful companies of the future are those that have already embarked on a long-term program of earning strong customer trust and loyalty, not to mention delight.

New Types of Relationships

Incorporating the new technology and dealing with rising customer expectations—not to mention changing demographics— have forced companies into the realization that they cannot fulfill any of their long-term strategies without completely revising their organizations. Hence the rise of the "virtual corporation."[3]

A virtual corporation is basically an organization that uses a combination of high technology and trained, adaptive workers to modify its form according to need in real time. In practice, as we read almost every day in the newspapers, what this means is a flattening of the organization by the reduction of middle management—replacing it with communications technology and databases, wider spans of control for senior management, and decision-making empowerment of line workers.

That's inside the company. Outside (and even that difference begins to disappear as the company becomes "edgeless") the company, virtualization means stronger linkages, even interpenetration, with vendors all the way up the supply chain, and distributors and retailers all the way down the distribution channel. Ultimately, it also means recruiting the customer into this "metaenterprise" for joint value creation as he or she is not only the first cause but the ultimate judge of all products and services created, as well as increasingly the first service rep, the assembler, even increasingly the product designer. One need only look at the celebrated case of furniture maker IKEA to see how a company can be transformed through collaboration with its customers. This collaboration is certain to grow richer with the advent of the World Wide Web.

Given all of those responsibilities—most of them taken on gladly because of the immediate and tangible rewards for doing so—the customer enters into a new kind of relationship with the vendor, a relationship that has been described as *co-destiny*. Everyone else, from raw materials refiners to local distributors, share that common destiny as well. Each commits enormous quantities of time, resources, and most of all trust that the other players on the team will do their part and make the entire project an enduring success.

As the top, center, and bottom of all of this activity, the customer is now in a unique position. But with customer success comes responsibilities. As we just discussed, the customer must divulge critical information in order that the product can be "mass-customized" for his or her specific desires. So, too, is there a commitment to spend considerable amounts of time in training (from videos for new car owners and weeks of classes for computer workstation owners to educational software on the Internet and teaching people to use a bank) in order to make the best use of the product or service. And, finally, when all this is done there is the implied commitment, after all this expenditure of time, money, and trust, to stick with the vendor for a long time to come.

This last commitment is not icing on the cake; rather, it lies at the very heart of the new economy. As competition grows fiercer in almost every market, and as manufacturing costs rise to meet the demand for ever smarter, ever more customized products, profits are getting squeezed. At the same time, with the rise of mass-customization, the very notion of product "models" fades into a continuous blur of capabilities offered by the company. The differences between products and services blur as well, with products being created like services on demand. Even inventories begin to disappear. What replaces them all is the enduring relationship between the customer and the vendor. The former secure in the knowledge that his or her needs will be perfectly fulfilled anytime and anywhere, and the latter rewarded with revenues from the sale to that customer of incremental improvements stretching out over years, even an entire lifetime.

THE NEW CUSTOMER METRICS

As we said in the previous chapters, and will say again in the ones to come, little of the emerging scenario described above can be captured by traditional financial documents. The old-fashioned company that continues to cherry-pick customers may look good in its current revenues and earnings but be doomed over the long term as the available pool of good customers is increasingly locked up by these new firms. Meanwhile, the company that is punished for having smaller margins may in fact be constructing a loyal and enduring customer base that will keep the company healthy for decades.

The task, then, for customer IC measurement is to find those measurements that best capture the new reality of effective and intelligent company-customer relations. Drawing from the earlier scenario, these indices and indicators cumulatively must capture the flow of relationships between a company and its current and potential customers:

A. *Customer Type*. What is the profile of a typical customer for the company's product, and how congruent is it to the company's long-term evolution? What is the potential for these customers to be "grown" as consumers of future company products and services? How do these customers compare in disposable income, education, age, and other factors compared to those of the competition? How large is the untapped pool of potential customers the company has yet to reach?

B. *Customer Duration.* What is the turnover rate of the current customer base? What is the average time a customer has been a loyal purchaser from the company? How do these two indicators compare with the industry average? How often is contact made? In consumer products, what is the rate of multigenerational customers? In industrial products, is the company a sole source or one of many? What information-sharing and educational systems—newsletters, Web page, magazines, customer events—are in place for sharing information with the customer?

C. *Customer Role.* What role does the customer play in product design, manufacture, delivery, or service? What is the value added by this participation and collaboration? What comparable programs are in place at the company's strategic partners, suppliers, distributors, and retailers?

D. *Customer Support.* What independent programs, facilities, and technologies are in place to assure the highest level of customer satisfaction and success? What is their value? How is the rest of the company organized toward front-line customer service? What is the value creation of those "captive" operations? What is the correlation between the company's investment in customer service and support versus increased levels of customer satisfaction?

E. *Customer Success.* What are the levels of customer success according to such metrics as annual purchase rate, annual purchase amount, customers with and without complaints, new and established customers, gender, income, profession, nationality, age?

You can see that if we were able to multiply A, B, C, D, and E, we would create a kind of "customer attraction index" that would offer clues to how close we are to full customer success.

Short of that we could create a five-axis chart that would show the strengths and weakness of the company in each of these areas. For example:

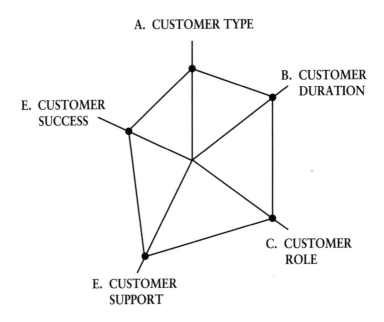

A. CUSTOMER TYPE

B. CUSTOMER
DURATION

E. CUSTOMER
SUCCESS

C. CUSTOMER
ROLE

E. CUSTOMER
SUPPORT

THE SKANDIA CUSTOMER FOCUS METRICS

Skandia, being a financial services firm, is no stranger to the art of maintaining close and enduring relationships with customers. When challenged to find new ways to measure this trait, the IC team reproted with the following long list:

1. *Market share (%).* Though market share alone is not a sufficient measure of a company's success with its customers, it is certainly a critical one. The company that gains and holds market share against the competition is obviously doing something that pleases customers. The subsequent indices and indicators can be seen as both creating this index and explaining it.

2. *Number of accounts (#).* This is a magnitude-setting measure, as the demands for good service (and the ability to deliver it) vary between a market with just a handful of customers and one with millions.

3. *Customers lost (#).* A critical one. In an era where there will be fewer and fewer available and good potential new customers, the loss of even a single current one is a singular defeat for the company. It represents the loss of years of time and money invested in developing that customer, and even more years of lost revenues.

4. *Telephone accessibility (%).*

5. *Policies without surrender (%).*

6. *Customer rating (%).* This group of three indices is Skandia's effort to capture the quality of its relationship with its customers. The first is a narrow-focus way of sampling the customer's daily interface with the firm. The company, the agent, the manager, that is not there on the other end of the line is never going to be able to provide total customer service. The second index is the view from the opposite perspective: How many customers, after a long period of frustration, have finally given up? The last is right down the middle: a statistical survey of customers to gauge their overall satisfaction dealing with the company.

7. *Customer visits to the company (#).*

8. *Days spent visiting customers (#).* These two measures are complementary. Together they show the degree of direct personal interaction between customers and representatives of the company. Apart, they show how those interactions are weighted.

9. *Market coverage (%).* This is not only a financial measure but a kind of opportunity index. It also provides a sense of how completely Skandia reaches its potential customer base.

10. *Vacancy rate (%).* Though unique to one of Skandia's real

estate businesses—that of managing property investments for clients—it does suggest the usefulness of tangential indices. In this case, a high vacancy rate would suggest that Skandia was not doing a good job of managing those properties and thus has not provided adequate value to its shareholders.

11. *Gross rental income/employee ($).*
12. *Number of contracts (#).*
13. *Savings/contract ($).*
14. *Points of sale (#).*
15. *Number of funds (#).*
16. *Number of fund managers (#).*
17. *Number of internal IT customers (#).*
18. *Number of external IT customers (#).*
19. *Number of contracts/IT-employee (#).*
20. *Customer IT literacy (%).* This is an interesting index because it turns the table around. Most companies are so focused upon their own IT prowess that they forget that their customers must also reach a certain IT competence threshold in order to remain successful customers.

A UNIVERSAL CUSTOMER IC METRIC

Obviously, many of Skandia's customer IC measurements are unique to the financial services industry, though many can be mapped over directly into such fields as real estate and insurance. As for manufacturers, service providers, and retailers, a closer inspection suggests that many of the indices and indicators need merely to be translated into product units, sales personnel, product returns, and complaint rates. Here are some possibilities:

1. Market share (%)
2. Number of customers (#)

3. Annual sales/customer ($)
4. Customers lost (#)
5. Telephone or electronic accessibility (%)
6. Average duration of customer relationship (#)
7. Average customer size ($)
8. Customer rating (%)
9. Customer visits to the company (#)
10. Days spent visiting customers (#)
11. Customers/employees ($)
12. Frontline employees (#)
13. Frontline management (#)
14. Average time from customer contact to sales response (#)
15. Ratio of frontline contacts to sales closed (%)
16. Satisfied customer index (%)
17. Rate of repeat customers (%)
18. Points of sale (#)
19. IT investment ($)
20. IT investment/service and support per customer ($)
21. Number of internal IT customers (#)
22. Number of external IT customers (#)
23. Number of contracts/IT-employee (#)
24. Customer IT literacy (%)
25. Support expense/customer ($)
26. Service expense/customer/year ($)
27. Service expense/customer/contact ($)

Finally, note the subtle shift in perspective that has occurred from the previous chapter on financial IC. There, most of the measurements were in units of money, the rest in percentages. Here, in customer IC, there are fewer monetary measures, more percentages and ratios. Suddenly, a preponderance of numerical measures—number of contracts, number of funds, and so on. The further we move down our "house" of Intellectual Capital, the further we are from traditional financial tables, the less monetary and more "flow-based" are our metrics. And that stands to reason: As noted earlier, the IC measurements at this level are of primary use in the present for valuation by investors and strategic decision making by company executives. It is fresh, raw, and not yet converted into final value. Instead, to look at the list above is to see a company locked into an ongoing, ever changing marriage of value creation with its customers.

7

Real Work: The Process Focus

We now enter into controversial territory.

This focus deals with the role of technology as a tool for supporting overall enterprise value creation.

For a half-century now, ever since the first big mainframe computers from IBM, Univac, and Burroughs appeared on the scene, industry—and accounting—has had a love/hate relationship with computers and high technology. Love, though sometimes merely obsession, has been the dominant emotion of the two. Companies and organizations have spent hundreds of billions of dollars on electronic equipment designed to improve their efficiency and productivity.

Much of it has worked—one can hardly imagine a large modern enterprise being successful without computerized billing and payroll, desktop and laptop computers, electronic mail, and intranets. Without question, semiconductors, computers, and telecommunication have made companies faster and more adaptive, allowed them to produce products of higher quality, and extended their reach to heretofore unreachable global markets.

At the same time, this technology has also allowed for greater organizational flexibility. Thanks to telecommuting, teleconferencing, and other new tech-based activities, companies can now employ talent temporarily or for the long-term that until now would have been too expensive or out of reach.

Finally, this technology in the form of EDI, Web pages, inventory networks, and the like has made possible the new types of virtual company relations with suppliers, distributors, partners, and customers that are critical to survival in the new competitive environment . . . and needless to say, this environment is itself the product of the general assimilation of this technology.

Thus, we are all trapped in and the beneficiaries of an upward technological spiral that might be creating ever more wealth, productivity, leisure, health, extended life spans, education, and access to life-enhancing experiences.

WEEDS IN EDEN

Sounds great, doesn't it? Even miraculous. And the amazing part is that most of it is true. Even modern Luddites who prefer a world without technology still want their cave equipped with a telephone to call the ambulance to take them to a high-tech emergency room where doctors using computer-controlled patient diagnostic systems or linked with remote experts can stare at digital displays and heal their ills.

But what is missing from the above narrative is the cost of usage. And this cost, which totals in the hundreds of billions, perhaps even trillions, of dollars, stands as the most effective argument against measuring the value of technology in a business—and by extension, of measuring Intellectual Capital. For that reason, we need to look more closely at the nature of valuing technology tools.

Wrong Technology

Applying a new technology is always a crapshoot. Adopt a new invention early and you may get a decisive advantage over your competitors. But if that technology proves a bust, or, just as bad, fails to become the standard, then you may find yourself behind your more conservative competitors and short on the money you need to invest to catch up.

Now add one more ingredient to the mix: If you are big enough and can get in on a technology early enough, you may, by investing enough of your company's money and forcing/convincing your suppliers, distributors, retailers, and customers to do the same, almost guarantee that technology becomes the industry standard and that you win. On the other hand, if you miss, you will likely cripple yourself and every one of your business partners—and earn the hatred of your (ex-)customers forever.

Choosing the wrong technology is the nightmare of every corporate MIS manager; and choosing the wrong technology to put into a new product is the even greater fear of every product designer. Silicon-on-sapphire chips, bubble memory, DR-DOS, the PCjr . . . the list of dead-end technologies is a long one. Even the experts screw up: IBM thought it could leapfrog the rest of the semiconductor industry with a new X-ray lithography technology that promised finer lines on a chip's surface. The technology seemed inevitable. Twenty years and billions of dollars later it still does.

Similarly, the impending year 2000 computer clock disaster, which may ultimately cost computer owners tens of billions of dollars, is an example of a hidden industry-wide technological mistake.

What is especially pernicious about wrong technologies is that they usually punish the most progressive, risk-taking companies. Fearful, conservative companies never buy new inventions.

Wrong Vendor

The Macintosh sitting on my desk is the sole survivor of more than three hundred personal computer companies that started at the same time as Apple Computer—and even multibillion-dollar Apple may soon be a name as lost to history as Hudson or Pierce-Arrow.

The story of high technology is the story of failure. Most of the dozen mainframe giants of the 1950s are now gone. So, too, are the fifty semiconductor companies of the early 1960s, the one hundred or more calculator makers of the early 1970s, the two hundred disk drive manufacturers of the early 1980s, and the thousands of PC software design shops of the early 1990s. Most of the tens of thousands of young Web designers will soon be gone as well.

The stories of these industry shakeouts are reported and soon forgotten as the next tech gold rush draws the world's attention somewhere else. Who remembers the Osborne computer? The companies disappear into bankruptcy or merger and their employees rush off to the Next Big Thing, the dead company existing only now as just a line item in their résumés.

But that isn't the only place those companies still exist. They also live on in the products they sold by the millions to customers, customers who believed these products were the magic bullet to success. Now they are stuck with processing equipment that is expensive, incompatible, unrepairable, and, needless to say, obsolete—"orphans" is the industry parlance.

The care and feeding of orphan products is a major business. There is a vast gray market of dealers who provide discontinued parts to keep these items going. What is interesting about these orphan products is that many are quite useful, some even a better fit for a particular application than the design that won. Thus, the near-term disadvantages of an orphan product can be small. But long-term, with no trained service reps, hard-to-locate replacement parts, no upgrade path, and most of all, the daunting and expensive prospect of porting a whole body of software over to a different standard, orphans can be hugely expensive.

Wrong Application

This is the new technology bought for the wrong reasons. Typically it is the result of "magic bullet" thinking; that is, computers are good, so if we just buy a bunch of them they will fix our problems. In the most extreme cases, it is the problem of backward thinking: buy the computers, install them, and then rethink the company around them.

The classic case of wrong application, one that is pointed to in seemingly every new business book, is that of General Motors in the 1980s. GM has become the bête noire of the new literature precisely because it spent so much money (one estimate is $40 billion) on technology for its own sake, and because the results went so spectacularly wrong (robots at its Hamtramck plant injuring workers, smashing cars). What GM is not given enough credit for is having learned the lesson about making the technology appropriate to the need and then applying it at the NUMMI and Saturn plants.

But wrong applications don't have to be as spectacular or as misguided as GM's. The fact is that every business large and small has, at one time or another, been swept up in the latest technological craze and bought high-tech equipment without fully understanding the need it was supposed to answer. By the same token one can find in every business some kind of technology that is an improper fit to its application—voice mail that doesn't quite work, a computer network that is too powerful for its use, a workstation in the lab that nobody knows how to use. All of these are classified as assets to the firm, but in real-life use may actually be liabilities in their damage to productivity and in the hoarding of cash that might be used elsewhere.

Wrong Philosophy

This is the subtlest but most sweeping and expensive technology mistake—and the one from which the average company can do little to protect itself. One little remarked characteristic of the history of technology adoption is the fact that it is cyclical. For example, in the Grand March of computers through the corporation, at each stop—manufacturing, bookkeeping, management, marketing, sales—the first round of adoption is almost always an expensive failure.

The reason is always the same: The technology is always acquired with the misguided belief that it will simply supercharge existing activities. The result is an open-ended, *divergent* implementation philosophy in which success is measured less by results than by how much money is being spent on technology. This was, in fact, the reason the GM debacle became so huge: Computers and robotics became desirable for their own sake, not for their contribution to value creation—and thus, without any measure of success but themselves, took on a momentum that couldn't be stopped.

Billions of dollars have been wasted throughout the world in these misguided implementations of tech. In manufacturing, it was Computer-Integrated Manufacturing (CIM), the idea that one could simply computerize the entire manufacturing floor into a monolithic integrated whole. In management, it was Management Information Systems (MIS). Most recently, it has been Sales Force Automation (SFA). A lot of acronyms, for essentially the same thing: forcing the organization to adapt to its technology tools rather than the other way around. Many have also suggested this is also what is wrong with modern education: the belief that just one more computer will suddenly lead to a student renaissance.

The critical clue to what is wrong with these and other automation philosophies is their open-endedness. An open system has no end point, no established goal that allows for feedback, interim measurements, course correction, or any other navigational information to tell the company if it is on the right track or approaching its goals. Success, which is to appear one day as profits, is always just over the horizon, and inevitably requires a new generation of equipment to get there.

The general failure of each of these automation schemes in turn led the shrewdest of their victims to stop and rethink first principles. With the collapse of CIM, a number of companies looked around for alternative and more controllable ways to use technology. Here, the major Japanese manufacturers, which had never gone overboard on tech but instead used it as a supportive tool, offered a different philosophy. It was that precise and measurable performance goals, based on strategic intent and core competencies, must be set first and then technology incorporated into that process only when it was *appropriate* and could be shown to contribute to those goals.

Hence the rise of Total Quality Manufacturing, which has found echoes in Total Quality Management and Total Sales Quality. In this countervailing philosophy precise goals are set— for example, Motorola's Six Sigma (one failure per billion), or in sales, one qualified lead equals one closed sale—and the right technology (robots, laptop computers, sales information databases) brought to bear to reach them. The result is a closed, *convergent* system in which the company's performance can be measured as it goes, and misjudgments (because this philosophy only protects against big mistakes, not small ones) regularly corrected and the company's efforts put back on track.

RETHINKING INFRASTRUCTURE

This litany of what can go wrong with the implementation of new technology in a corporation is not designed to scare everybody away from infrastructural innovation. On the contrary, in today's competitive environment, the latest tools may be the only edge a company has.

However, it is designed to be a warning to those pursuing the Intellectual Capital model and seeking to codify the valuation of technology on its balance sheet. No IC model will work if one can pump it up merely by buying more computers than the competition. This is the structural version of Davidow's warning at the beginning of this book. If a firm can simply go out and purchase a new computer network for its employees, have it fail, and still record it as an Intellectual Capital asset, then something is very wrong.

The solution is to develop metrics for the Process Focus that recognize this concern and account for the four above-mentioned types of technology infrastructure mistakes. In other words, process indices that:

1. Value acquired process technologies only when they contribute to the value of the firm.
2. Track the age and current vendor support for company process technology.
3. Measure not only process performance specifications but actual value contribution to corporate productivity.
4. Incorporate an index of process performance in relation to established process performance goals.

Here is how Skandia began to deal with these issues in its early IC Annual reporting:

1. *Administrative expense/managed assets (#).* Note how few of these indices actually deal with monetary values but instead are ratios and a sizable number of simple values.
2. *Administrative expense/total revenues (#).*
3. *Cost for administrative error/management revenues (%).* This index is a measure of the efficiency of the company's performance by looking at the ratio of the cost of messing up. Needless to say, publishing this figure takes management courage.
4. *Total yield compared with index (%).* This measures how well Skandia's asset management program compares to the industrywide index.
5. *Processing time, outpayments (#).*
6. *Contracts filed without error (#).*
7. *Function points/employee-month (#).* These three are the nitty-gritty of company operations and the results are a test of the company's infrastructure.
8. *PCs/employee (#).*

9. *Laptops/employee (#).*
10. *Administrative expense/employee ($).*
11. *IT expense/employee ($).*
12. *IT expense/administrative expense (%).* These five build together to show the level of technology penetration into the daily work lives of employees (number 8, by the way, had a value of 1.28 at Skandia, suggesting an impressive five PCs for every four employees), and then how that technology overhead relates to the company's overall administrative performance efficiency development.
13. *IT staff/total staff (%).*
14. *Administrative expense/gross premium (%).* This is a measure of the overall process efficiency of the firm.
15. *IT capacity (CPU and DASD) (#).* For Skandia, this was basically a measure of the overall performance of its AS/400 system (166,300 trans/hour and 47 GB) and its PC local area network (14,055 MIPS and 199 GB).
16. *Change in IT inventory ($).* This is the amount the company spent on new IT equipment over the course of the year.
17. *Employees working at home/total employees (%).* This is an especially interesting metric, as it gives a glimpse of the future of telecommuting. It also is a check on how efficient that IT capacity is.
18. *IT literacy of employees (#).* This indicates how well the staff is using the organization's IT investment.

This is a good start, but it still falls short in light of the need to defend against misrepresentation of technology mistakes. Here are some indices that might help do that:

19. *Corporate quality goal (#).*
20. *Corporate performance/quality goal (%).*
21. *Contribution of IT inventory less than two years old/quality goal (%).*

22. *Cost of IT inventory less than two years old/increase in revenues (%).*

23. *Cost of IT inventory less than two years old/increase in profits (%).*

24. *Value of IT inventory discontinued by manufacturers ($).*

25. *Discontinued IT inventory/IT inventory (%).*

26. *Replacement cost of IT inventory (including incompatible software) discontinued by manufacturers ($).* Note that it is not always a bad thing to use obsolete equipment (if the parts can be found), especially if replacing it would be a huge expense. But it is crucial to acknowledge the existence of such equipment and all of the attendant problems (breakdowns, expensive repairs) that come with it.

27. *Value of IT inventory by manufacturers no longer in business ($).*

28. *Orphan IT inventory/IT inventory (%).* This is an overall look at the company's technological vulnerability.

29. *Replacement cost of orphan IT inventory (including incompatible software) (%).*

30. *IT capacity/employee (#).*

31. *IT performance/employee (#).* These are two that Skandia missed. They answer the critical question of just how much processing power resides in the hands of each employee.

Ultimately, the goal of all of these measurements is to present a usable perspective on how an enterprise uses its technology tools to create value. There are, of course, other perspectives, such as those suggested by Michael Hammer, Tom Davenport,[1] and especially Kaplan and Norton.[2] They, too, might generate their own unique measurements. But they, too, would still fit within the overall focus structure of the IC Navigator.

Real Future: The Renewal and Development Focus

With the Renewal and Development Focus we move out of the present and try to capture the opportunities that will define the company's future. You might say that we are in search of the new bottom line, the foundation of long-term sustainability.

The renewal and development indices lie at the opposite pole from the financials. Where the latter fix forever the immediate past performance of the organization, the Renewal and Development Focus attempts to cast outward into the immediate future by establishing what things the company is doing now to best prepare itself to grasp future opportunities.

Obviously there is almost no defense for titanic economic shifts or acts of God; and there is precious little a company can do to prepare itself for radical inflections in the market due to unanticipated new inventions. Success in responding to these cataclysms is usually due to the strength of the company's character and the resilience of its employees—that is, the company's ability to renew itself. And if those characteristics cannot be precisely visualized, we believe that the overall metrics of Intellectual Capital do as good a job as anything yet found to capturing their essence.[1]

WHERE THE FUTURE LIVES

But short of the world turning upside down, it *is* possible to identify areas of emphasis by which a company can ready itself for impending change and then actively promote its own renewal in response. Experience has shown there may be six such angles of perspective, and that accompanying each of them is a body of proven strategies for success. Here they are, along with suggested directions for more detailed investigation of potential indices.

Customers

What are the expected changes in the customer base in absolute numbers, demographics, buying patterns, income, education, age, and the like? What level of service are these customers receiving today from the company and what are their likely expectations for service in the future? What is the current level of customer educational support in terms of manuals, seminars, training programs, and so forth? What level of training and support—competence upgrading—will likely be necessary in the future given currently planned new products or services? What in-house service and support programs are under way to meet these needs? What research has been done for contractual delivery of these programs from outside alliances? What is the evolution of the customer's customer?

How regular and efficient are communications between the company and its customer base? How much is invested annually in these communications? What is the rate of use of this system by customers? What is the value of ancillary customer development and relationship programs (discounts for events, gift certificates, rebates)?

Attractiveness on the Market

How much is the company investing in market intelligence? What percentage of this targets current markets? What percentage targets new markets (that is, opportunity share)? What is the contribution of new markets (less than four years old) to company revenues and profits? What is the company's participation in industrywide programs—trade groups, task forces, standards commissions, government lobbying? What programs does the company have in place to track new inventions and new competitors? How much coverage does the company and its products receive in key trade publications? How are trademarks and brand images evolving?

Products and Services

How many new products or services does the company currently have in development? What is the historic likelihood of innovations under development coming to market? What is the speed at which this historically occurs? What is the historic contribution of a typical new product or service to revenues and profits? What is the historic life expectancy of new products or services? What is the anticipated life expectancy of new products or services under development? What is the current ratio of new products or services (less than two years old) to the entire company catalog?

What is the total investment in new product/service development? What are the percentages devoted to basic research, product design, applications? What is the commitment (money, staff, contractors) to supporting (manuals, seminars, etc.) and servicing the new products/services?

What are the number and age of the company's patents? What are the number and age of patents licensed by the company? What is the duration of the terms on those licenses? How many patents does the company have pending? Filed? In preparation for filing? What are the company's current revenues from the licensing of its patents?

Strategic Partners

How much does the company invest in strategic partnership development and networking? How many company employees are stationed at partners' facilities? Vice versa? What is the cost and capacity of the electronic data interchange system between the company and its partners? What is its rate of use? What corporate information is restricted from exchange with partners? What percentage of company products is designed or built by partners? What is the company's investment in competence upgrading programs between it and its partners? How does it assess and nurture its partnershipping operations?

Infrastructure

What is the value, age, and life expectancy of the company's organizational capital support tools? What capital acquisitions does the company anticipate in the next three years? What percentage of company revenues and profits will be contributed by these purchases? What is the configuration and value of the company's current management information system, sales information system, CAD/CAM system, process control network, intranet, E-mail system, and all other data communications networks? What is the current capacity of these systems? What is the expected load on these systems? Hw many new organizational capital tools emerge every year as a transformation of human capital? How much is recycled?

Employees

What is the current average education of the company's employees? How many MBAs? How many nontechnical Ph.D.'s? How many scientific and engineering graduate degrees? How many new competence profiles are added annually? What is the average amount, in hours, of training per employee per month? What is the goal? What is the current and planned growth in value added per employee? What is the current and planned investment in employee recruiting programs? How many different cultures are represented in the employee populations? What cross-generational programs are in place? What cross-cultural relations programs are in place?

THE SKANDIA REPORT

In 1994, when Skandia developed its IC Annual Report, the company reported the following renewal and development indices:

1. *Competence development expense/employee ($)*. Note that this is a targeted measure, emphasizing those activities by the firm designed to make the individual employee more productive in his or her area of expertise. This is distinguished from number 11 below, which also includes other forms of employee development, including basic communication skills, time management, and the like.
2. *Satisfied employee index (#)*. This measure of employee's attitudes and motivation is based upon qualitative reviews taken of Skandia employees every twelve months.
3. *Marketing expense/customer ($)*.
4. *Marketing expense/managed asset ($)*. These two measures are designed to capture the company's commitment to marketing by using two approaches.
5. *Share of "Method and Technology" hours (%)*. This refers to the systematic packaging of experiences for future sharing and recycling.
6. *Share of training hours (%)*.
7. *Share of development hours (%)*. These three measurements show the amount of time the company devotes to three areas it believes crucial to its continued competitiveness.
8. *R&D expense/administrative expense (%)*.
9. *IT expense/administrative expense (%)*.
10. *Training expense/employee ($)*.
11. *Training expense/administrative expense (%)*.

12. *Premium from new launches (%)*. This is Skandia's way of measuring whether its new services are continuing to effectively revitalize the firm, not only filling the gaps left by declining products but expanding upon them.

13. *Increases in net premium (%)*. This one tests whether those new services are, from a revenue standpoint, better than the ones that preceded them.

14. *Business development expense/administrative expense (%)*. This measures the company's commitment to building structural capital for the future. Note that some of the previous measures each compare one facet of the company's R&D program to the overall administrative overhead of the firm. This overall index is thus an early warning meter to capture when Skandia's commitment to future development is threatened by the current internal inertia toward ever greater bureaucracy and the impediments it creates to change.

15. *Share of employees under age 40 (%)*. This ratio offers a glimpse of the company's ability to maintain its current levels of energy and intensity, as well as its ability to move into the future without losing its character and operating philosophy through attrition. It also gives a hint to values of the workforce. However, it is important to note that this measurement also works in the other direction: A company too skewed toward callow youth may be lacking the perspective of veterans and the continuity of corporate philosophy needed to build and maintain an enduring enterprise.

16. *IT development expense/IT expense (%)*.

17. *IT expenses on training/IT expense (%)*. These two measurements look inside the corporate IT department to determine whether it is properly investing in its own future.

18. *R&D resources/total resources (%)*. Finally, this is an overall measure of how much commitment the company is making to its future renewal and development.

MEASURING READINESS

It is interesting to compare how Skandia, independently attempting to find the metrics that would best capture its readiness for the future, managed to cover to various degrees each of the six strategic areas described earlier.

With the Skandia indices as our model, let's now reinvestigate those areas and propose a list of tentative measurements for a hypothetical organization:

1. *Competence development expense/employee ($).* Needless to say, as this is a future-oriented focus that deals only marginally with types of company products, many of Skandia's measures can be ported over with little or no translation to our model.
2. *Employee Empowerment Index (#).* Note that in measuring subjective assessments by employees and customers, Skandia went to independent outside polling services. This seems a good idea for any company and should probably be incorporated into any code that emerges for reporting IC.
3. *Renewal expense/customer ($).*
4. *Renewal expense/product line or service ($).*
5. *Share of "Method and Technology" hours (%).*
6. *Share of training hours (%).*
7. *Share of development hours (%).*
8. *Employees' view (Empowerment Index) (#).*
9. *R&D expense/administrative expense (%).*
10. *Intrapreneurial employees/total staff (%).*
11. *Time to establish a new foreign office (#).*
12. *IT expense/administrative expense (%).*
13. *Training expense/employee ($).*
14. *Training expense/administrative expense (%).*
15. *Business development expense/administrative expense (%).*
16. *Share of employees under age 40 (%).*
17. *IT development expense/IT expense (%).*

18. *IT expenses on training/IT expense (%).*
19. *R/D resources/total resources (%).*

Now, to this basic Skandia list, consider some more indices derived from the six strategic areas:

20. *Customer base (#).*
21. *Average customer age (#); years of education (#); and income (#).*
22. *Average customer duration with company in months (#).*
23. *Average customer purchases/year ($).* Needless to say, on this measure and the three that precede it, the company is making public a considerable amount of what is traditionally proprietary information. Whether the company chooses to do so is, on balance with its growing need to be open with its investors, an important decision it must make. It is our belief that as the customer base gets more bound up with the company, this information will seem less private over time.
24. *Training investment/customer ($).* This accompanies the two indices for support and service expense/customer found in the Customer Focus section.
25. *Investment in new customer service/support/training programs ($).*
26. *Direct communications to customer/year (#).* Measures how often the company actually communicates (newsletters, direct contact, magazines, press releases, and so forth) per year.
27. *Average contacts by customer/year (#).* This looks the other way, at how responsive and involved the company's customers are.
28. *Non-product-related expense/customer/year ($).* This measures the ancillary customer-related investments, from bonuses and gifts to information gathering.

29. *New markets development investment ($).*

30. *Industry development investment ($).* Of these two measures, the former captures the company's investment in developing new markets for its products and services, the latter looks at the company's participation in industry-wide efforts such as trade organizations. This second measure should include such things as the salaries of executives on loan to associations, and comparable contributions.

31. *Investment in competitive intelligence programs ($).*

32. *Investment in strategic partner development ($).*

33. *Employees based at partners' facilities (#).*

34. *Partners' employees based at company's facilities (#).*

35. *Total value of EDI system ($).*

36. *Upgrades to EDI system ($).*

37. *Capacity of EDI system (#).*

38. *Company products (or components) designed by partners (%).*

39. *Percentage of customer training, service, and support provided by partners (%).*

40. *Common training programs of company and partners ($).*

41. *New products currently in development (#).*

42. *Company historic rate of new products reaching market (%).*

43. *Historic life expectancy of new products (#).*

44. *Ratio of new products (less than two years) to full company product family (%).*

45. *R&D invested in basic research (%).*

46. *R&D invested in product design (%).*

47. *R&D invested in applications (%).*

48. *Investment in new product support and training ($).*

49. *Number of company patents (#).*

50. *Average age of company patents (#).*

51. *Patents pending (#).*

The next group of indicators measures the infrastructure of the company, its reach, how well the company is keeping it up-to-date, and most important, how much it actually contributes to the company's value. The last, obviously the most difficult to measure, is vital because it recognizes that in the lean company of the future, *every* operation must explicity show its value creation, its EVA (Economic Value Added), to the enterprise. It is also a check on the installation of technology for its own sake.

52. *Value of the company's management information system ($)*
      Capacity (#)
      Upgrades ($)
53. *Contribution of MIS system to corporate revenues ($)*
54. *Value of the company's engineering design system ($)*
      Capacity (#)
      Upgrades ($)
55. *Contribution of engineering design system to corporate revenues ($)*
56. *Value of corporate sales information system ($)*
      Upgrades ($)
      Capacity (#)
57. *Contribution of sales information system to corporate revenues ($)*
58. *Value of process control system ($)*
      Capacity (#)
      Upgrades ($)
59. *Contribution of process control system to corporate revenues ($)*
60. *Value of corporate communications networks ($)*
      Capacity (#)
      Upgrades ($)
61. *Contribution of corporate communications network to corporate revenues ($)*

That is a lot of metrics. And certainly, time and experience will whittle down some of these as irrelevant or impossible to measure (though it will likely also add a few we've missed). It may even be possible, as with the Customer Attraction Index, to boil all of these indicators and ratios down into a single Opportunity Index.

Nevertheless, precisely because the future is the future of the firm, and because identifying current trends that will affect the future is so difficult and elusive, it stands to reason that the more measurements, the more likely one is to find the handful that prove decisive in capturing a useful perspective on the organization's future opportunities. The task of renewal and development is to find the idle untapped potential of an organization's intangible assets. So for now, asking a lot of different questions is the best way to get there.

Real Life: The Human Focus

We've saved the most dynamic factor for last.

Whereas all of the different sections of the Navigator interact with one another to various degrees, only the human factor interpenetrates the others, serving as the active agent operating upon all the others. Without a successful human dimension to a company, none of the rest of the value creation activities will work, no matter how sophisticated the technology. An unhappy company is a worthless company; an enterprise without values has no value.

CAPTURING HUMANITY

But measuring the Human Focus is also the most difficult part of the IC model—which explains all of the research, from human resource accounting to Nobel laureate Gary Becker's work *Human Capital*. There is no simple way to measure what is in the heads and hearts of managers and employees. There are no columns of numbers to add, no gauges to check, no meters to read. Affixing a value to behavior or motivation is an entirely different matter from, say, accounting for total sales or determining computer capacity.

For that reason, any metrics dealing with personnel by necessity must be:

1. *Well-reasoned,* so as not to measure something apparently important but ultimately meaningless.
2. *Well-designed,* so as not to pick up the noise of other subjective variables.
3. *Teleological,* because the very act of choosing metrics reflects the company's own human resource biases. Therefore, the measures must be chosen so as to reflect not only where the company is but where it should be. Some must also change to reflect the changing values of society.

That's only the beginning of the challenges associated with measuring human motivations and capabilities. The international Organization for Economic Cooperation and Development (OECD) has spent years investigating how to best measure human capital in a rapidly changing information economy.

Recognizing that "economic survival of enterprises, and the employability and earning power of individuals, depend more and more on learning as the basis for agile adaptation," two OECD researchers, Riel Miller and Gregory Wurzburg have studied the obstacles to measuring productivity and the value of employee education.[1]

Their conclusion: "For all the importance of the knowledge and skills of the workers as factors in performance, not only are the means for measuring them remarkably crude; they are also rigidly determined by the certifying institutions."[2]

Not a good sign. Miller and Wurzburg then go on to list "three substantial barriers [that] stand in the way of more effective approaches to measuring and valuing human resources in more knowledge- and skill-intensive economic activities."[3]

Here are the three they found (italics added):

One is *lack of transparency in the costs of labor,* and particularly of upgrading the qualifications of experienced workers. As continuous upgrading becomes a routine part of human-resource management, labor costs expand beyond the usual wage and non-wage expenses (social charges, pension and health costs), to include the direct costs of training (course fees, training material) as well as indirect costs (such as the value of production forgone while workers are off the job, and that lost as workers practice and perfect what they have learned).

Yet the definition and measurement of these attendant costs, and the extent to which they are reported for statistical or tax reporting purposes, are highly variable. . . .

A second problem is the *difficulty of measuring the productive capacity*—the knowledge, skills and abilities—that workers acquire through further training and/or experience on the job. Methods and institutions for undertaking this type of "in-progress assessment" remain underdeveloped. . . .

Even when qualifications can be measured, there is a third problem in *reflecting an economic value* for them. The barriers here are found in a number of forms. Enterprises cannot capitalize training costs or the stream of benefits from upgraded qualifications of workers to carry them on the balance sheet of their financial reports. . . .[4]

Miller and Wurzburg go on to conclude that this "absence of more sophisticated means for measuring and valuing human resources, particularly the qualifications acquired through experience and training, can heighten the risk of misallocation of resources."[5]

The solution? Happily, Miller and Wurzburg point to the measure of Intellectual Capital as one way to capture some of this elusive information. But, they add, it isn't enough, unless the definitions of labor costs are made more precise and the measure of employee competence more systematic. The OECD itself has taken on the first obstacle, working with the Australian government to develop a manual to systematize the collection of training statistics. For the larger task of actually measuring productive capacity, Miller and Wurzburg point to the skills evaluation programs developed by governments, universities, and private corporations throughout the world, such as France's Bilan des Competences, Canada's Assessment of Prior Learning, and New Zealand's National Qualifications Framework. (It is interesting to note that, despite the many public statements by government officials such as Clinton labor secretary Robert Reich about the need for worker retraining, no such comparable national framework for qualifications exists in the United States.)

The real message of the OECD research is a warning: The measurement of human capital in an organization is a process fraught with peril, one that risks wild inaccuracies and fraud unless there is a general agreement on intent, metrics, and value. Agreement on definitions and goals must occur at the beginning. The establishment of metrics can be aided by work done in other fields, notably skills training, sociological research, and polling. Finally, with these two factors in place, Intellectual Capital can provide the format for presenting the results—but only if the measurements chosen are congruent with the true values of the firm.

THE NEW WORKER

If this isn't challenge enough, there are still other, tectonic, shifts taking place in the labor force and the organization that will challenge those definitions and metrics even as they are being created—and will demand a whole new layer of information in order to capture their dynamics.

The new, virtual corporation is edgeless in regards to not only its strategic partners but also its employees. In this age of cellular telephones, the Internet, and corporate co-destiny, the traditional employment population, once centralized in corporate buildings at a few sites and sharing a common philosophy, lifestyle, and community, has now been scattered across the landscape. It now exists in numerous subgroups with their own experiences, mores, and rules. So, where is the human capital?

The number of these subpopulations grows by the year. The current list includes several.

Office Goers

These are the workers and managers who still travel each day to the office or the factory. They face the traditional challenges of living near the facility and dealing with peripheral matters such as commuting. At first glance, this group would appear to be the one part of the labor force that remains essentially unchanged. However, early research suggests this is not true at all.

For example, the work environment will change as many companies, no longer needing a large physical presence, will radically downsize to the point that even the office employees of a giant firm will find themselves in a small-company setting. Moreover, sociological studies have found that, because they are more visible, office goers are more likely to be stuck with rotten jobs than their invisible, work-at-home counterparts. Office goers are also more likely to find themselves in the role of ground station, fielding questions and offering support to their outlying peers. And finally, there are the more subtle resentments that come from being the person who must live near the office, who must drive in to that office every day, and who is stuck with all the scut work—all the while knowing that others are living where they choose, working out of their dens, and escaping all but the important jobs.

Telecommuters

This is the new breed of employee who, through advances in telecommunications and computers, is freed to work from home or some outlying office . . . and, moreover, getting to choose where that workplace will be.

This sounded good in principle when telecommuting was first tried at the beginning of this decade, but experience has now shown us the downside. Working in your bathrobe in the den sounds terrific, until the workday suddenly becomes a continuous twenty-four hours per day. And there is the screaming baby and the barking dog and the Federal Express guy banging on the door.

Most of all, there is the sense of isolation. If the office goer feels put upon and under surveillance, the telecommuter feels forgotten. With companies physically downsizing, this creates the added wrinkle for telecommuters of not having a headquarters at all. Now, out there in orbit, the telecommuter may feel there is no center to the company at all. And some research already suggests that this isolation can result in a lack of loyalty, sinking morale, even a diminishment in creativity.

Road Warriors

At the extreme, these same advances in computing and telecommunication, especially related to portability, have made possible a new subculture. Road warriors are company salespeople, middle managers, and executives who have essentially jettisoned both the corporate office and the home office and, through an electronic umbilicus of skypagers, cell phones, and laptop computers, have embarked on a nearly perpetual road trip. A typical road warrior may only visit the office four or five days each month and the rest of the time be on the road. It can be a relentless existence, but the road warrior motto is: If you are not on your edge, you take up too much space.

Road warriors are in the paradoxical situation of being detached from the company while still being at the very center of its operations and value creation. Road warriors rarely feel detached from the operations of the company, but often feel alienated from its daily life. This ambivalent situation grows even more severe with time, as road warriors have increasingly begun to develop their own language, lifestyle, and culture.

Corporate Gypsies

These come in two forms. The first, and smaller, group are those employees who through the nature of their work (such as product design) find themselves working at the facilities of one of the company's suppliers, strategic partners, or customers. In some respects these individuals are isolated from their company even more than telecommuters, having to operate daily within another, and often quite different, corporate culture.

The larger group of corporate gypsies—and their numbers swell every year—is the population of contractors, part-timers, consultants, and temporary employees who swell the corporate ranks and often bear all of the responsibilities of a full-time employee, yet are never fully part of the firm. In some companies, this group may account for 70 percent or more of the workforce. The contributions of these individuals may be enduring or evanescent, their time with the company measured in hours or decades. Tomorrow they may take their skills to the competition, or start a competing company of their own. Most of all, their loyalty to the company is problematic: Some may feel deeply involved with their (temporary) employer, others may feel an allegiance only to their peers, to their employment service, or just to themselves.

Ultimately, a third type of corporate gypsy may appear, buoyed by the Internet. These will be individuals who operate at the extreme edge of short-term, contract employment—that is, they will sell their skills to scores of companies each week, working for none of them for more than a few minutes before moving on. They will be the cyber equivalent of longshoremen or day laborers, queuing up each morning to await the call, going "off" to work for a brief period, gathering their pay, and returning to await the next call. These electronic gypsies will hold no more loyalty to any employer than they do the stores at which they shop—yet their contribution to the company's value may, on occasion, be enormous.

*　　*　　*

All of these employee populations coexist in the modern virtual corporation. The result is a level of chaos and mixed loyalties unimaginable in the traditional corporate organization chart. Replacing the standard hierarchical organization will be something resembling a bull's-eye: concentric rings of real and pseudo-employees emanating out from the small core of full-time—often lifetime—employees who hold the key knowledge of the organization, maintain its philosophy, pass on its myths, and will be the cultivators of long-term relationships with employees and partners.

These critical employees, some of whom will be office goers, but many also road warriors and telecommuters, will represent the heart of the company, and will as such be nearly irreplaceable. They will be the front-liners in value creation. They will know that—and as a result will present a unique challenge to management, one akin to that of coaching athletes who are more valuable to the organization, and better paid, than the coach.

The next ring outward will be those full-time and full-time part-time employees who are of the firm, but not necessarily in it—telecommuters, road warriors, long-time contractors, and the like. Their sole contact with the company may be through computer screens, telephones, newsletters, and the occasional company gathering at some large off-site location because the company itself has shrunk too small to hold them.

This group may be able to switch jobs at the punch of a computer key, spend more time at the neighborhood coffeeshop with their telecommuting competitors than with their own fellow employees, and feel no great pressure to follow the instructions of a boss who is a continent and four time zones away. To lead this group will require an entirely different set of skills, one that makes heavy use of electronic communications (television programs, Web pages, daily corporate newspapers), social events, and special bonus and reward systems. You might call this a *networking leadership competence.*

Finally, on the periphery are the gypsies, a group whose successful management lies less with instilling loyalty than by interesting projects, fast payment, alternative reward schemes, and recognition. This type of management may prove to be closer to customer relations than to corporate human resources.

Looking at this complicated structure, it quickly becomes obvious that no single leadership style will work with all of these constituencies. Rather, it may take three or four different approaches, each with different tools and skill sets, many of them unlike anything currently taught in management school. These different staff groups will themselves require different structures and reward systems. And that in turn will require different types of senior leadership.

MEASURING PEOPLE NEAR AND FAR

Put all of this together—the problem of measuring current employee competence, combined with radically new work styles and management models—and the obstacles to measuring the human Intellectual Capital of a company become almost overwhelming.

Nevertheless, it is our belief that it can be done. The challenge is to set down now the basic metrics for employee and manager productivity, as well as for the infrastructure needed to serve those groups, then grope our way forward in the years to come, identifying the changes described above as they occur and establishing common techniques to measure them.

Here is how Skandia made a start in 1994:

1. *Leadership Index (%).*
2. *Motivation Index (%).* These first two indices were the product of a measurement system, the FLINK index, cre-

ated by Skandia in one of its units. FLINK is composed of those factors that Skandia believed contributed most to the company's market success and profitability:

- Satisfied customers
- Satisfied salespeople
- Motivated and competent staff
- Quality-assured and effective administrators

Goals were set in each of these areas, questions devised, and employee interviewed. Based upon these polls, Skandia was able to establish ratios for the quality of management and employee motivation in relation to the established goals.

3. *Empowerment Index (of 1,000) (#).* For this index, Skandia hired SIFO, the Swedish Institute of Public Opinion Research, to survey company employees to determine how much control they feel over their daily work. The particular factors SIFO looked at were:

- Motivation
- Support within the organization
- Awareness of quality demands
- Responsibility versus authority to act
- Competence

Note the overlap in some areas with entry 1. This redundancy recognizes that employee motivation is an important value in itself but is also a factor in the larger question of employee independence.

4. *Number of employees (#).*
5. *Number of employees/number of employees in alliances (%).* This is the leveraging indicator of the networked organization.
6. *Employee turnover (%).*

7. *Average years of service with company (#).* As noted earlier, this figure is of great importance. Employee turnover, especially in the core group of the company, is a threat to sustained organizational capital value.

8. *Number of managers (#).*

9. *Number of women managers (#).* At first glance, this may appear to be simply one more manifestation of political correctness, a sop to interest groups monitoring the employment of women. But the fact is that the new corporation, with its diverse management needs, will require personality types, life experiences, and management styles that are unprecedented in the middle corporate ranks. Thus, diversity, more than just an end in itself, may prove to be a vital competitive factor.

10. *Training expense/employee ($).*

11. *Average age of employees (#).*

12. *Share of employees under age 40 (%).* These two measurements represent an attempt by Skandia to capture the rate at which the company refreshes its talent pool. Combined with numbers 9 and 12, the company presents an overall look at the demographics of the company, combined with how well company veterans are kept up to speed on the latest technologies and techniques.

13. *Time in training (days/year) (#).*

Studying Skandia's Human Focus factors, two things become apparent. The first is that all of these measurements can be directly ported over to other industries. That's the good news; the bad news is that here, in the most complex part of the corporate Intellectual Capital equation, the Skandia team has come up with the shortest list of indicators and indices of the five. This is partly due to the sheer complexity of the topic; but it might also be the result of Skandia looking only at its current employment metrics as opposed to what is likely to arise in the future, i.e., mapping performance as well as values.

Let's begin with the Skandia list and then, using the different employment constituencies described at the beginning of this chapter as our model, construct a body of additional measurements that both capture the dynamics of those different groups and measure how well management is coping with the differing demands of these groups.

1. *Number of full-time permanent employees.* We begin by distinguishing each of the constituencies. This first group, which includes most office goers, telecommuters, and road warriors, establishes the core group of critical veteran employees and how effective the company is at keeping them and rewarding them.

2. *Full-time permanent employees as percentage of total employment.* This shows the size of the core group; too small and the company may not be able to perpetuate itself, too large and the company may be carrying too much labor overhead.

3. *Average age of full-time permanent employees.* In this core group (as opposed to the company overall), youth may not be an advantage. The conveyance of corporate philosophy is typically best done by older employees.

4. *Average years with company of full-time permanent employees.*

5. *Annual turnover of full-time permanent employees.* This is a critical factor. A company bleeding core veterans is one at great risk.

6. *Per capita annual cost of training, communication, and support programs for full-time permanent employees.* This core group requires, and expects, special treatment. This measures the company's commitment to keeping these veterans happy.

7. *Full-time permanent employees who spend less than 50 percent of work hours at a corporate facility.* This is the telecommuter/road warrior/off-site employee measure. A

high percentage in this index suggests a different corporate organization than a small one.

- Percentage of the total workforce.
- Percentage of full-time permanent employees.
- Per capita annual cost of training, communication, and support programs. This is likely to be a large amount, given the cost of portable communications equipment, laptop computers, and so forth.

8. *Number of full-time temporary employees.* This group of indices measures the next constituency.

- Percentage of the total workforce.
- Average years with company of full-time temporary employees.

9. *Per capita annual cost of training and support programs for full-time temporary employees.* This is a measure of the company's commitment to all of its employees.

10. *Number of part-time employees and non-full-time contractors.*

- Percentage of the total workforce.
- Average duration of contract.

11. *Per capita annual cost of training, communication, and support programs for part-time employees and non-full-time contractors.* This measure is likely to become increasingly important in the years to come as companies compete for the attentions of short-term talent.

Now for measuring the new management:

12. *Percentage of company managers with advanced business degrees.*

- Advanced science and engineering degrees.
- Advanced liberal arts degrees. The first two are pretty standard, but the last is something new. Once considered a handicap, a liberal arts degree may provide a new set of skills of great value to a fast-moving, adaptive firm.

13. *Percentage of company managers of different nationality than the company registry.* Diversity does not include only gender. In global competition, global management is a competitive edge.

14. *Company managers assigned to full-time permanent employees.*

- Assigned to full-time employees who spend less than 50 percent of work hours at a corporate facility.
- Assigned to full-time temporary employees.
- Assigned to part-time employees and non-full-time contractors. This group of indices measures the company's recognition of its different constituencies and then its commitment of management time to them.
- Number of different languages and cultures/total staff.

Is this enough to capture the human Intellectual Capital of the modern corporation? No, but it pushes the process a little bit further. Here, more than any other part of the Navigator, practice and experience will make the difference. The nuances of human behavior and motivation are notoriously tricky. The best run company can suddenly suffer a devastating crisis of spirit that will overwhelm every other company value, yet won't be reflected even on this extended list for months or more.

Will we ever find this X factor? Well, we know where to look: out in the no-man's-land where the Human Focus rubs against each of the other four focuses: customers, process, financial, and renewal and development. It is the dynamics of these interfaces from which the fine balance between people and institution is set. And this balance becomes more difficult to achieve and this kind of "values mapping" more important as the organization enters more culturally diverse global markets or into alliances with a more diverse array of partners.

But finding the X factor is not the same as anticipating its changes. That may always remain impossible. But there may be ways to react to these changes as soon as they appear . . . as we'll see in the final chapter of this book.

10

All Together Now

Before we tie everything together, let's take a look at how one dedicated individual has systematically built an IC program at his well-known company—and has already seen positive results on the balance sheet. It is an interesting glimpse at not only what can be gained financially and competitively from such a program but also the pragmatic realities of putting such a program in place.

Gordon Petrash was happily working in global business management at the Styrofoam insulation division of Dow Chemical in 1992 when he was approached by the company's vice president of R&D.

"He told me that the Dow's management was realizing that the company was underutilizing and underleveraging its vast collection of patents," Petrash recalls. "Then he put his hand on my shoulder and said, 'Gordon, go get more money from them.'

"And that's how it started."

The choice of Petrash for the job was hardly arbitrary: His division, Fabricated Products, was one of the few parts of the company managing its intellectual property (i.e., its patent portfolio) well.

Petrash took the job willingly but not without some trepidation. Dow, he already knew, was a veritable patent machine. But the magnitude of the process surprised him. The company was spending $1 billion annually on research and development, its

139

4,000 researchers generating several hundreds of new patents each year in support of the firm's 2,000 products. Over the years this had created a company portfolio of more than 29,000 patents.

Just the tax obligations on such a portfolio cost Dow more than $170 million over an average ten-year period.

Despite the sheer magnitude of the challenge, Petrash knew that Dow had to find a way to better manage all those patents. "If I had to choose one idea that acted as a catalyst," he would tell the *European Management Journal* in 1996, it is this quote from the futurist Joel Barker:

> Corporate intellectual properties will be more valuable than their physical assets in the 21st century.
>
> There are some companies that were highly profitable only a few years ago and are barely surviving today. There are companies that were not around ten years ago that have leapfrogged the industry leaders. . . . I believe there is a direct correlation between how the intellectual assets of a corporation have been managed to its financial success.

The good news was that Dow had been a pioneer in keeping precise records on this portfolio. For thirty years the company had maintained, in Petrash's words, "an R&D knowledge system"—a database that could allow the portfolio to be searched by key word, subject, author, etc.

"Dow had vast arrays of knowledge and information silos," Petrash recalls. "The problem was not the depth of the knowledge or depth within the silos but how they connected with one another. That had always been the real limitation of knowledge management in Dow."

Petrash set out to change that. He gathered a team of a half-dozen people from throughout Dow, and they set out to research the subject. They quickly learned that "good companies have always managed intellectual capital very well," Petrash says.

"They just didn't express that fact. As it turns out our research found citings in the literature about 'intellectual capital' as far back as the 1960s. But that was it; only now are people creating a language to better articulate what this fuzzy stuff is."

The first step was to appreciate where Dow was in regards to its own intellectual asset management. In 1993 a group of senior executives at the firm joined forces to determine how the company currently managed those assets (labeled the "is") and to articulate where the company ought to be in this effort (the "should").

Petrash and his team took this "should" vision and simplified it into a six-phase summary model for the management of intellectual assets:

1: Portfolio—The articulation in simple terms of the company's current intellectual assets. "This assembling of the patent portfolio was not easy," Petrash would later write. "We had to identify all of the properties, determine if they were still active and find an internal business or cost center that would take ownership and pay the costs appropriate with pursuing or maintaining the property. A lesson learned in this phase of aligning properties to a business was that identifying the business that benefited from the value of the property or that sponsored it made the process much simpler."

2. Classification—"In this step we determined the 'use' of the property. Each business classified all of their properties into three major categories: a) the business is 'using,' b) the business will 'use' and c) the business will 'not use.' Each of these classifications had additional detailed designations, i.e., license, abandon, etc." Petrash's team classified all 29,000 Dow patents in this way.

3: Strategy—"This is taking your portfolio and knowing how you are utilizing it and integrating it into the business strategy. An objective of this phase is to identify the intellectual asset gaps between the business strategy and the capabilities of the existing intellectual asset portfolio.

"This is where resources that are targeted toward creating intellectual capital can be focused."

4: Valuation—Working with consulting firm A. D. Little, Dow developed the "Tech Factor Method," a comprehensive intellectual property valuation program for use with licensing, opportunity prioritization, and taxes.

5: Competitive Assessment—Dow used a number of popular competitive technology assessment tools, but the team found the one most effective for its purposes had been used by the company for more than fifteen years: "the patent tree." This was a technique by which Dow could organize its own patents vis-à-vis those of its competitors in order to evaluate such factors as dominance, breadth of coverage, blocking, and opportunity openings.

6: Investment—With an understanding now of the value of its existing intellectual assets, its competitive situation, and its goals, Dow can now proceed to fill in those gaps between its portfolio and its strategy. This is currently being done either through in-house development or through external acquisition.

And with that, the cycle began again with a reevaluation of the company's portfolio in light of these investments, newly developed assets, and the changing competitive environment.

Constructing such a model and implementing it were two different things. First there was the matter of staffing. By 1996, Petrash had reorganized his core team, now ten people, to act as the hub of a large network of one hundred intellectual asset "teams," composed of three to five people each, scattered throughout the giant company. The annual budget for this operation is currently $1 million.

But building an IA reporting structure was only part of the challenge. There was also the critical matter of politics: How to convince senior management in a short time of the usefulness of such a program while still pursuing long-term goals? This became even more critical as Petrash and his team studied the work being done at places like Skandia and realized they needed to expand their perspective beyond intellectual property assets to an all-encompassing model of Intellectual Capital. "It really opened up our perspective," Petrash says.

The first step, the team realized, was education. "We needed to be able to put the very complex world of intellectual assets into terms businesspeople could understand. We wanted to be able to tell the whole story on a single sheet of paper. It was a long journey, but we were finally able to do that."

The next challenge was to find some short-term successes to prove the value of the program to management. As it turned out, the six-phase program, by locating forgotten intellectual properties, identifying new ones to acquire, and scrutinizing the strengths and weaknesses of the competition, immediately bore fruit. Just through culling out useless patents, the project saved the company $40 million in tax maintenance over a projected period. "Money gets credibility," says Petrash with satisfaction.

That was just the beginning. Says Petrash, "We continually look for successes, publicize them, and work to make them become best practices here at Dow."

Meanwhile, the team never lost track of its larger goals. While management was enjoying the savings from the new intellectual property program, Petrash and his crew were expanding their charter to include "a new larger long-term strategy to better measure and manage Dow's Intellectual Capital."

The IA program proved to be a useful springboard. Says Petrash, "We said to ourselves, 'Hey, if it works for patents, why not everything else?'" Thus, the patent tree evolved into the "knowledge tree," containing all of Dow's intellectual assets. So, too, the team found, could the six-phase model be applied to other intangibles at Dow, including know-how, secrets, and employee knowledge.

All of these other efforts have remained largely under wraps, even within Dow. But that will soon change: In late 1997, Petrash and his team plan to publish Dow's first Intellectual Capital report. It will likely be the first such document by a U.S. company.

Petrash and crew have only begun. "We have started advocating for Intellectual Capital on a wider basis at Dow," he says. "It's moving slower than I'd like, but we are definitely moving that way. Sometimes it's just a matter of telling the story five different ways ten different times in order to get support. But we'll get there."

For Gordon Petrash, Intellectual Capital has become more than merely the source of a new revenue stream for his employer; it is also a way to stay on top of a rapidly changing world. "The way I see it," he says, "the audience for this is employees first, shareholders and other stakeholders second.

"Tracking Intellectual Capital is a way for the company not just to find and put to use its hidden assets but also to reconnect with its people. The changing competitive environment has forced every company to shred the social contract it had with its employees. And in the process, many firms have lost track of the real value of their 'human capital.' IC measurement will be a regular reminder."

Petrash also believes that for his program to work, it must ultimately render itself obsolete. "In the future," he says, "the whole world of knowledge management should not be an applied science as it is now, but an integrated science.

"We've been down this path before. Here in the chemical industry Dow used to have a entire Department of Safety, with its own staff that managed a population of safety managers located in every one of our plants. Now that department doesn't exist. Why? Because it served its purpose by getting its ideals integrated into every part of the company. Every employee is now a safety manager.

"The same is true with IC management. If it can only operate as a separate operation, it will eventually wither and die. But it will be successful if every employee becomes his or her own knowledge manager and teacher. And it will have truly done its job when the CEO also becomes the company's chief knowledge and learning officer.

"That will take some time, but we are making continual progress toward that goal."

THE SKANDIA PRECEDENT

We've now investigated in depth each of the five Focus Areas in the Navigator and in the process tried to establish a body of indicators designed to illuminate driving forces for corporate value in a dynamic and timely way.

Now we need to synthesize all of these parts into a single, coherent whole. In the process we will be making the first attempt at a universal statement of Intellectual Capital. We have no illusions that this will be the final form, but we hope it will be a valuable starting point for dialogue and, ultimately, codification into reporting standards.

One last point. Among the very important contributions Hubert Saint-Onge and Charles Armstrong have made to Intellectual Capital theory is the idea of a *value platform*. To understand what he means by this, look at the accompanying illustration (page 146).

It is Saint-Onge's and Armstrong's contention, and we believe a valid one, that it is not enough to simply have the three present-time factors—Human, Structural, and Customer—standing alone as independent sources of Intellectual Capital. Rather, they must be in *alignment* so as to complement one another. At the intersection of the three factors lies the value platform, the source of all value creation by the organization.

There are two important messages that immediately arise from this model. The first is that corporate value does not arise directly from any of its Intellectual Capital factors, but only from the interaction between *all* of them. Second, and just as important, is that no matter how strong an organization is in one or two of these factors (say a powerful and dynamic organization or a brilliant staff), if the third factor is weak or, worse, misdirected

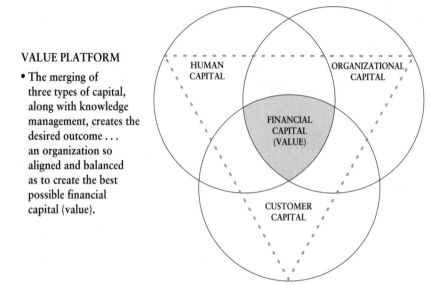

VALUE PLATFORM

• The merging of three types of capital, along with knowledge management, creates the desired outcome ... an organization so aligned and balanced as to create the best possible financial capital (value).

Source: Hubert Saint-Onge, Charles Armstrong, Gordon Petrash, Leif Edvinsson

(say, the wrong customer base), that organization has *no* potential to turn its Intellectual Capital into corporate value.

It is a chilling thought and a strong warning.

TOGETHER FOR THE FIRST TIME

Now, on to the IC report.

Such a report represents two major steps. First, it brings together the new body of indices and indicators created off the original financial services industry–oriented Skandia metrics, as well as those devised independently in the creation of this book. But just as important, this is also the first enterprise-level IC reporting model.

When the team at Skandia prepared the 1994 IC Annual Report, it faced two constraints. One was the sheer difficulty of gathering unprecedented information in a company with no experience at doing so. Thus, some measures, useful as they might have been, were simply abandoned because there was no way to get the relevant data. Second was the requirement to be pedagogical: The mission of the first IC Annual Report was to not only provide information about the company but also to show that the model worked. Because of that, the report did not aspire to take IC reporting beyond individual units and subsidiaries, using each to visualize one of the factors.

Thus, the Skandia measurements of the previous chapters were actually cobbled together from a half-dozen different division reports. So, for example, in the renewal and development chapter the "Competence development expense/employee" figure was actually measured only for the wholly owned subsidiary SkandiaBanken Fonder, while "Share of 'Method and Technology' hours" came from the internal service unit, Skandia Data Information Technology.

Because of that, the first step in creating a universal annual IC report must be to pull all of these parts of Skandia in 1994 together for the first time into a single IC format. Here it is:

FINANCIAL FOCUS
1. Fund assets ($)
2. Fund assets/employee ($)
3. Income/employee ($)
4. Income/managed assets (%)
5. Premium income ($)
6. Premium income resulting from new business operations ($)
7. Invoicing/employee ($)
8. Customer time/employee attendance (%)
9. Insurance result/employee ($)
10. Loss ratio compared to market average (%)
11. Direct yield (%)
12. Net operating income ($)
13. Market value ($)
14. Market value/employee ($)

15. Return on net asset value (%)
16. Return on net assets resulting from a new business operation ($)
17. Value added/employee ($)
18. IT expense/administrative expense (%)
19. Value added/IT-employees ($)
20. Investments in IT ($)

CUSTOMER FOCUS

1. Market share (%)
2. Number of accounts (#)
3. Customers lost (#)
4. Telephone accessibility (%)
5. Policies without surrender (%)
6. Customer rating (%)
7. Customer visits to the company (#)
8. Days spent visiting customers (#)
9. Market coverage (%)
10. Vacancy rate (%)
11. Gross rental income/employee ($)
12. Satisfied Customer Index (%)
13. Number of contracts (#)
14. Savings/contract ($)
15. Surrender ratio (%)
16. Points of sale (#)
17. Number of fund managers (#)
18. Number of funds (#)
19. Number of internal IT customers (#)
20. Number of external IT customers (#)
21. Number of contracts/IT-employees (#)
22. Customer IT literacy (%)

PROCESS FOCUS

1. Administrative expense/managed assets (#)
2. Administrative expense/total revenues (#)

3. Cost for administrative error/management revenues (%)
4. Total yield compared with index (%)
5. Processing time, outpayments (#)
6. Applications filed without error (#)
7. Function points/employee-month (#)
8. PCs/employee (#)
9. Laptops/employee (#)
10. Administrative expense/employee ($)
11. IT expense/employee ($)
12. IT expense/administrative expense (%)
13. Contracts/employee (%)
14. Administrative expense/gross premium (%)
15. IT capacity (CPU and DASD) (#)
16. Change in IT inventory ($)

RENEWAL AND DEVELOPMENT FOCUS

1. Opportunity share (%)
2. Competence development expense/employee ($)
3. Satisfied Employee Index (#)
4. Marketing expense/customer ($)
5. Marketing expense/managed asset ($)
6. Share of "Method and Technology" hours (%)
7. Share of training hours (%)
8. Share of development hours (%)
9. R&D expense/administrative expense (%)
10. IT expense/administrative expense (%)
11. Training expense/employee ($)
12. Training expense/administrative expense (%)
13. Premium from new launches (%)
14. Increases in net premium (%)
15. Business development expense/administrative expense (%)
16. Share of employees under age 40 (%)
17. IT development expense/IT expense (%)
18. IT expenses on training/IT expense (%)
19. R&D resources/total resources (%)

HUMAN FOCUS
1. Leadership Index (%)
2. Motivation Index (%)
3. Empowerment Index (of 1,000) (#)
4. Number of employees (#)
5. Employee turnover (%)
6. Average years of service with company (#)
7. Number of managers (#)
8. Number of women managers (#)
9. Training expense/employee ($)
10. Average age of employees (#)
11. Time in training (days/year) (#)
12. IT-literacy of staff (#)
13. Employees working at home/total emplyees (%)

The question to ask about this list is whether it successfully maps over from the division or subsidiary to the company as a whole. We believe it does. And that paves the way for our universal IC report as a medium for visualizing in numbers and images the value of companies as a whole.

REPORTING IN HUMAN SCALE

But now we have a problem: The Skandia IC report contains ninety-one different measurements. That's a daunting number, and even assuming that companies will institutionalize the measurement of these indices and use considerable computing power to do so, it will remain a monumental task.

Now, if we compile all of the new indices and indicators we've created, including those translated from the Skandia originals, we come up with 164 measurements, not counting subcategories. In the future, when companies are completely wired and are monitoring all of their activities in real time, then tracking nearly two hundred variables may be feasible, even desirable. But right now it is hard to imagine why any contemporary company would be willing to make such a commitment in time and money to do so.

So, what we need to do first with our new universal IC reporting standard is to cut out the redundant and less important indices, as well as those that will be inordinately difficult to measure, so that we are left with a list comparable in length and complexity to the Skandia original. The others can be preserved for future elaboration as the measurement systems become more sophisticated, and used now only by companies willing to invest in value-added information—or even, conceivably, be used in a supplementary document.

We also need to look for patterns of new value creation to help us further our refinement. To help keep us on track, let's take a quick look at the latest IC taxonomy, as developed by researchers Göran and Johan Roos.

Here, then, is our best guess as to what the structure of a universal IC report should be:

The Intellectual Capital Report

FINANCIAL FOCUS

1. Total assets ($)
2. Total assets/employee ($)
3. Revenues/total assets (%)
4. Profits/total assets ($)
5. Revenues resulting from new business operations ($)
6. Profits resulting from new business operations ($)
7. Revenues/employee ($)
8. Customer time/employee attendance (%)
9. Profits/employee ($)
10. Lost business revenues compared to market average (%)
11. Revenues from new customers/total revenues (%)
12. Market value ($)
13. Return on net asset value (%)

14. Return on net asset resulting from new business operations ($)
15. Value added/employee ($)
16. Value added/IT-employees ($)
17. Investments in IT ($)
18. Value added/customer ($)

CUSTOMER FOCUS

1. Market share (%)
2. Number of customers (#)
3. Annual sales/customer ($)
4. Customers lost (#)
5. Average duration of customer relationship (#)
6. Average customer size ($)
7. Customer rating (%)
8. Customer visits to the company (#)
9. Days spent visiting customers (#)
10. Customers/employees ($)
11. Revenue generating staff (#)
12. Average time from customer contact to sales response (#)
13. Ratio of sales contacts to sales closed (%)
14. Satisfied Customer Index (%)
15. IT investment/salesperson ($)
16. IT investment/service and support employee ($)
17. IT literacy of customers (%)
18. Support expense/customer ($)
19. Service expense/customer/year ($)
20. Service expense/customer/contact ($)

PROCESS FOCUS

1. Administrative expense/total revenues (#)
2. Cost for administrative error/management revenues (%)
3. Processing time, outpayments (#)
4. Contracts filed without error (#)
5. Function points/employee-month (#)

6. PCs and laptops/employee (#)
7. Network capability/employee (#)
8. Administrative expense/employee ($)
9. IT expense/employee ($)
10. IT expense/administrative expense (%)
11. Administrative expense/gross premium (%)
12. IT capacity (CPU and DASD) (#)
13. Change in IT inventory ($)
14. Corporate quality performance (e.g., ISO 9000) (#)
15. Corporate performance/quality goal (%)
16. Discontinued IT inventory/IT inventory (%)
17. Orphan IT inventory/IT inventory (%)
18. IT capacity/employee (#)
19. IT performance/employee (#)

RENEWAL AND DEVELOPMENT FOCUS
1. Competence development expense/employee ($)
2. Satisfied Employee Index (#)
3. Relationship investment/customer ($)
4. Share of training hours (%)
5. Share of development hours (%)
6. Opportunity share (%)
7. R&D expense/administrative expense (%)
8. Training expense/employee ($)
9. Training expense/administrative expense (%)
10. Business development expense/administrative expense (%)
11. Share of employees under age 40 (%)
12. IT development expense/IT expense (%)
13. IT expenses on training/IT expense (%)
14. R&D resources/total resources (%)
15. Customer opportunity base captured (#)
16. Average customer age (#); education (#); income (#)
17. Average customer duration with company in months (#)
18. Educational investment/customer ($)
19. Direct communications to customer/year (#)

20. Non-product-related expense/customer/year ($)
21. New markets development investment ($)
22. Structural capital development investment ($)
23. Value of EDI system ($)
24. Upgrades to EDI system ($)
25. Capacity of EDI system (#)
26. Ratio of new products (less than two years) to full company product family (%)
27. R&D invested in basic research (%)
28. R&D invested in product design (%)
29. R&D invested in applications (%)
30. Investment in new product support and training ($)
31. Average age of company patents (#)
32. Patents pending (#)

HUMAN FOCUS
1. Leadership Index (%)
2. Motivation Index (%)
3. Empowerment Index (#)
4. Number of employees (#)
5. Employee turnover (%)
6. Average years of service with company (#)
7. Number of managers (#)
8. Number of women managers (#)
9. Average age of employees (#)
10. Time in training (days/year) (#)
11. IT-literacy of staff (#)
12. Number of full-time/permanent employees (#)
13. Average age of full-time/permanent employees (#)
14. Average years with company of full-time permanent employees (#)
15. Annual turnover of full-time permanent employees (#)
16. Per capita annual cost of training, communication, and support programs for full-time permanent employees ($)
17. Full-time permanent employees who spend less than 50

percent of work hours at a corporate facility; percentage of full-time permanent employees; per capita annual cost of training, communication, and support programs

18. Number of full-time temporary employees; average years with company of full-time temporary employees
19. Per capita annual cost of training and support programs for full-time temporary employees ($)
20. Number of part-time employees/non-full-time contractors (#)
21. Average duration of contract (#)
22. Percentage of company managers with advanced degrees:

- Business (%)
- Advanced science and engineering degrees (%)
- Advanced liberal arts degrees (%)

There are now a total of 111 main indices. That's still a sizable number, but we believe well within the capabilities of a modern company with computer-based information systems. Here are the other fifty-one indices, by focus, that were put aside for future or current ancillary use. In perusing this second list, you may find disagreements with us over choices. That's good, because the whole point of this exercise is to provoke reflection and dialogue with the goal of eventually settling upon a list of measures to be captured by the standard IC report:

FINANCIAL FOCUS
1. Market value/employee ($)
2. IT expense/administrative expense (%)

CUSTOMER FOCUS
1. Telephone electronic accessibility
2. Rate of repeat customers (%)
3. Points of sale (#)

4. Number of internal IT customers (#)
5. Number of external IT customers (#)
6. Number of contracts/IT-employees (#)
7. Customer IT literacy (%)

PROCESS FOCUS
1. Administrative expense/managed assets (#)
2. Total yield compared with index (%)
3. Employees working at home/total employees (%)
4. Contracts/employee (%)
5. Cost of IT inventory less than two years old/increase in revenues (%)
6. Cost of IT inventory less than two years old/increase in profits (%)
7. Value of IT inventory discontinued by manufacturers.
8. Replacement cost of IT inventory (including incompatible software) discontinued by manufacturers ($)
9. Value of IT inventory by manufacturers no longer in business ($)
10. Replacement cost of orphan IT inventory (including incompatible software) (%)
11. Contribution of IT inventory less than two years old to quality goal (%)

RENEWAL AND DEVELOPMENT FOCUS
1. Marketing expense/product line ($)
2. Share of "Method and Technology" hours (%)
3. Average customer purchases/year ($)
4. Investment in new customer service/support/training programs ($)
5. Average contacts by customer/year (#)
6. Investment in competitive intelligence programs ($)
7. Investment in strategic partner development ($)
8. Company products (or components) designed by partners (%)

9. Percentage of customer training, service, and support provided by partners (%)
10. Common training programs of company and partners ($)
11. New products currently in development (#)
12. Percentage of customer training, service, and support provided by partners (%)
13. Common training programs of company and partners ($)
14. New products currently in development (#)
15. Company historic rate of new products reaching market (%)
16. Historic life expectancy of new products (#)
17. Number of company patents (#)
18. Value of the company's management information system ($)

   Capacity (#)

   Upgrades ($)
19. Contribution of MIS system to corporate revenues ($)
20. Value of the company's engineering design system ($)

   Capacity (#)

   Upgrades ($)
21. Contribution of engineering design system to corporate revenues ($)
22. Value of corporate sales information system ($)

   Upgrades ($)

   Capacity (#)
23. Contribution of sales information system to corporate revenues ($)
24. Value of process control system ($)

   Capacity (#)

   Upgrades ($)
25. Contribution of process control system to corporate revenues ($)
26. Value of corporate communications networks ($)

   Capacity (#)

   Upgrades ($)

27. Contribution of corporate communications network to corporate revenues ($)

HUMAN FOCUS

1. Managers assigned to full-time permanent employees (#)
   Assigned to full-time employees who spend less than 50 percent of work hours at a corporate facility (#)
   Assigned to full-time temporary employees (#)
   Assigned to part-time employees and non-full-time contractors (#)
2. Per capita annual cost of training, communication, and support programs for part-time employees and non-full-time contractors
3. Percentage of company managers of different nationality than the company registry

COMMON VIEWPOINTS

As we noted at the beginning of this book, Skandia's is only the most advanced among IC reporting programs at companies throughout Scandinavia. Knowledge company expert K-E Sveiby has studied and reported on three of the other most progressive of these companies: WM-data, PLS-Consult, and Celemi.[1]

According to Sveiby, WM-data has been measuring its intangible assets for more than a decade, even including a section on intangibles ("How Our Capital Is Managed") in its annual report since 1989. WM-data uses a reporting format devised by Sveiby himself, dividing its Intellectual Capital (or as it calls them, intangible assets) into three categories: internal structure, external structure, and employee competence.

PLS-Consult, a Danish management consultancy, has reported on its intangible assets in its annual reports since 1993. PLS-

Consult also divides its intangible assets into three classes: customer capital, consultants' intellectual knowledge, and the company's organizational knowledge.

Celemi, by comparison, has gone as far in IC reporting as any company outside Skandia. Beginning in 1995, the company, which develops and sells training tools, has included a "Knowledge Audit" in its annual report. This audit also divides intangible assets into three categories: our customers, our organization, and our people. Within each of these three categories are three subcategories: growth/renewal, efficiency, and stability—the nine groups containing the twenty-three indicators that constitute Celemi's Intangible Assets Monitor. They are as follows:

OUR CUSTOMERS

Growth/Renewal
1. Revenue growth
2. Image enhancing customers

Efficiency
1. Change in sales/customer

Stability
1. Repeat orders
2. Five largest customers %

OUR ORGANIZATION

Growth/Renewal
1. IT investment % value added
2. Organization enhancing customers
3. Product R&D % value added
4. Total investment in organization % value added

Efficiency
1. Change proportion of administrative staff
2. Sales per administrative staff growth

Stability
1. Administrative staff turnover
2. Administrative staff seniority years
3. Rookie ratio

OUR PEOPLE

Growth/Renewal
1. Average professional experience in years
2. Competence enhancing customers
3. Total competence of experts in years
4. Average education level
5. Efficiency
6. Value added per expert
7. Value added per employee

Stability
1. Expert turnover
2. Expert seniority in years
3. Median age of all employees in years

It is interesting to note how these firms, coming from the same philosophical source but pursuing their ends independently, have come up with reporting models that closely resemble Skandia's. Further, the more sophisticated these reports, as in the case of Celemi, the more it appears that the "auditors" find themselves facing the same core questions and developing almost identical reporting formats and indicators.

Though these efforts certainly don't provide full validation of the IC reporting model, they do suggest that when a company decides to look into the measurement of its intangible assets it will inevitably follow a similar path. First dividing those assets into some combination of structural, human, and customer capital. Then linking those factors on one hand to the future development of the company and on the other to the financial accounting of the firm. Then creating some kind of navigational format to move about these factors. Finally, coming up with a body of indicators that, whatever their titles, measure the same body of intangible assets.

This commonality, in turn, supports the notion that Intellectual Capital not only exists and can be measured but that the measurement process is itself common to different organizations.

AN IMPETUS TO ADOPTION

The response to the presentation so far will likely vary with the profession of the reader. The senior executive may well react that sure, it would be great to have all of this information, but do we really want to share it with the competition? Especially in those areas where we've really screwed up. Say what you will about the old balance sheet, it did hide a lot of mistakes.

The chief information officer or MIS director may be shaking his or her head and saying, do you know how much it will cost to install an IS system to capture all of this data? It would have to be all custom too, because there's nothing off the shelf that matches it.

The accountant is probably feeling more than a little ambivalent. On the one hand, this new IC model is an apparent threat to everything he or she has spent years learning and perfecting. At the same time, it represents an extraordinary new business opportunity that will restore the lost relevancy the entire profession is experiencing. With the rise of Intellectual Capital, accounting firms, big and small, have a unique opportunity to help their clients establish, run, and validate computer-based IC reporting systems.

The most competitive, and thus desirable, of these systems will be those that link together the existing databases of the company (sales information, management information, production control, and the like), probably through an intranet-based architecture and Java applets, to quickly capture information that is already there. In many companies that existing pool of IC information may represent a majority of the IC measurements . . . which answers the concern of the CIO.

Moreover, the biggest accounting firms will be able to develop proprietary IC reporting software that simplifies this data-gathering task still further. That should calm the biggest doubts of the folks in IT.

That leaves senior management and its fears of opening the company books too far. The simple answer to that fear is that a closer look at the above list will show that much of this information is already found in the footnotes and appendices to the modern earnings statement and balance sheet. Of those that remain, none expose the nature of any of the company's proprietary product developments, the names of key customers, strategic partners, and so forth. That leaves only the fear that some critical flaw in the company's performance or behavior, heretofore camouflaged, such as the sudden departure of a number of key employees or a rise in customer dissatisfaction, will suddenly be spread out on the table for public scrutiny.

First of all, it is hard to feel much sympathy for management that sees such problems and is not immediately making herculean efforts to fix them. Second, in the age of hundreds of vertical trade magazines, newsletters, and the Internet, any company that believes it can keep these secrets for long is kidding itself.

There is also a philosophical answer to the senior executive's concern. It is that the modern, virtual corporation demands openness and the sharing of once proprietary information. In the best companies, that information is already being shared with frontline employees, suppliers, distributors, retailers, and strategic partners. It will also soon be shared with customers to enlist their participation and creativity. That is a huge population of people—and if a company believes it can stop there, throwing up an information firewall to keep that knowledge from the rest of the world, it is delusional. The last constituency, investors, is going to request such information, and it will get it somehow, from customer communications to tapping the company's own intranet. And if investors get that information, you can be sure the world will get it too.

Finally, there is one last, definitive, reason why companies will adopt IC reporting and share this inside information with the world: because they can. Smart, successful companies will recognize that IC reporting gives them a competitive advantage when it comes to valuation, and therefore they will jump on the bandwagon. Companies that fear this exposure for whatever reason may try to resist, but they will look churlish and secretive (which will be, in fact, true) and will be instantly at a disadvantage in the investment market to their more open competitors. As a result, they will have no choice but to go along . . . kicking and screaming perhaps. But the long-term effect of exposing and curing their failings will undoubtedly prove salutary.

AGREEING ON STANDARDS

That leaves a final step: standardization. In the United States (and by extension, Asia and Latin America), that means FASB and the SEC; in Europe it means the Accounting Council of the EU.

Will these organizations accept IC reporting as an additional, and more immediate, measure of value? To date there is no definitive answer. However, there is evidence—conferences on IC on both sides of the Atlantic sponsored by these groups—that both of these organizations recognize the growing importance of IC metrics.

Part of this recognition stems from the realization that the current accounting model is inadequate in the modern economy. That new tools must be developed to enhance that model. And that IC reporting is ultimately about nonfinancial indicators leading to (and thus impacting) financial returns. But just as important there is the recognition that the growing interest in

Intellectual Capital reporting could create a de facto standard outside the control of these governing bodies—rendering them increasingly superfluous and opening the doors to widespread abuse. This would place the governing bodies in the position of not fulfilling their mandate.

For both these reasons, it is likely that some sort of industry-wide, government-sponsored standardization of IC measurement will occur around the end of the century. And, needless to say, the speed of this standardization will be largely paced by how fast this model is ratified by industry at large. It is our belief that this will occur very quickly, a chain reaction of a few progressive firms raising investor expectations, which in turn will force more recalcitrant firms to follow suit. It will also likely be spurred by the SEC and large institutional shareholders with long-term interests such as pension funds.

But it will only occur quickly if certain immediate obstacles are overcome. We have already mentioned the skepticism of certain orthodox interest groups (senior management, IT, accounting) to some aspect or another of IC reporting. And we have also given reasons why we think those obstacles will be met.

Just as much of an obstacle is the actual practice of IC reporting. Establishing the reporting system and putting into place the right technology to process it will not be simple, even with the help of outside consultants (that is, big accounting firms) and new applications programs. It will also require a mind-set change among those who administer it.

Some theorists of Intellectual Capital, notably Annie Brooking, founder and managing director of The Technology Broker (UK), have already begun to investigate the internal challenges posed by a company's IC audit.[2]

Brooking's model does not include an actual final IC report or particular indices. Rather, her work is inside the company: focusing upon how managers should use IC measurement to change their own self-awareness about their companies' Intellectual Capital value. This in turn serves as the philosophical underpinning for a long-term IC measurement and reporting program. Brooking's message is that IC measurements are not only for the outside world but also for the company to better understand and enhance itself.

It is Brooking's belief that it is vital for a company, before beginning an IC audit, to identify its strategic intent. Otherwise, she says, the firm could spend huge sums and waste innumerable hours measuring every company intangible, conducting psychometric tests on employees, and counting up the value of every intellectual property right—and end up with "an immense amount of knowledge . . . [that] would help us generate statistics that may or may not be useful information." Moreover, given the complexity of human beings, without goals, "the process would never ever conclude."[3]

In other words, IC measurement, too, must be convergent.

The metrics of the IC report implicitly provide many of these goals. But they are not the whole story. For corporate managers, the value of IC measurement, says Brooking, takes many forms, including that it:[4]

1. *Validates the organization's ability to achieve its goals.* Brooking argues that strategic planning and goal setting sometimes fail not because of a faulty plan but because the company discovers too late that it doesn't have the intangible asset resources needed to succeed. An IC audit can identify those gaps.

2. *Plans research and development.* There is perpetual confusion in R&D planning between the creation of patents and new designs and the development of know-how. The former is often for defensive purposes and is expensive to maintain, while the latter is often the source of real benefit to the company. An IC audit not only distinguishes the company's commitment to each, but in the case of know-how, helps the company understand what competitive advantages it truly has for value extraction.

3. *Provides background information for reengineering programs.* "When organizations decide to downsize or reengineer, decisions must be made concerning human assets," writes Brooking. "These decisions are often made in a vacuum, as human assets are evaluated in an ad hoc fashion. . . . An intellectual capital audit will . . . [ensure] that neither of these processes inadvertently divests the organization of valuable capability and know-how."[5]

4. *Provides focus for organizational education and training programs.* Continuous training is the watchword of the modern corporation, but few companies have a clue as to what part of their employee training programs actually enhance productivity and which are misdirected and worthless. By understanding its Intellectual Capital assets, a company can redesign its training programs to best enhance those assets.

5. *Assesses the value of the enterprise.* Here Brooking's work connects with this book as she suggests that "an intellectual capital audit provides in-depth knowledge of the intangible assets of the organization, which can be used to support the tangibles, giving analysts and financiers an information-rich perspective on the organization."[6] To this one can only add that the best way to provide this information to "analysts and financiers" (not to mention individual shareholders and customers) is to present it in a standardized format that is common across industry—as this allows for better comparison and bench learning.

6. *Expands the organizational memory.* This takes two forms, according to Brooking. The first is the use of the audit to identify key resources and individuals so that they can be properly used, rather than the company spending huge sums to perpetually reinvent those skills. The second is the recognition that the company's institutional memory is itself an intangible asset (i.e., organizational capital) that must be nurtured and regularly measured.

What Annie Brooking's work brings to the theory and practice of Intellectual Capital is its opening and closing argument. For the modern corporation, understanding the value of its intangible assets is a critical factor to its success. This understanding enables the company to know where its strengths lie and to access them quickly in a fast-moving competitive and networking environment. Conversely, it also shows the company its underlying weaknesses, and thus enables it to fix these problems before they emerge as a dangerous operating problem. In other words, IC audits make the company more alert, competitive, and thus more sustainable and successful.

That's the opening argument in support of a company committing the time, talent, and resources to begin measuring the value of its Intellectual Capital. At the other extreme, the closing argument comes after the company has made that initial IC audit and is now contemplating an ongoing program of publicly reporting its IC assets. Now, Brooking's research argues that IC reporting not only will help the company increase its worth in the eyes of partners and investors, but by keeping it on track toward its internal structural goals, also make the company more efficient, profitable, and competitive. In other words, IC audits make a company more valuable not only to the world but to itself. And that should answer any doubts a company could have.

REVITALIZING THE AUDIT

One of the most disheartening discussions we've had in the last year came in a not-for-attribution conversation with an attorney from a major U.S. accounting firm. Shaking his head, the attorney said, "During the early nineties, when all of the mergers and acquisitions were taking place, you almost never heard about disputes over corporate audits. I mean, here were billions of dollars moving back and forth, major companies being bought and sold, unfriendly takeovers—and nobody arguing about accuracy of the balance sheets.

"Well, we in the industry took a lot of pride in that. It was only later we realized that the reason our work was never in dispute was because nobody gave a shit about us anymore. We had become irrelevant to the process. And we've been trying to recover ever since."[7]

The accounting industry today finds itself in a crisis of purpose. Just at the time when it has perfected the processes for obtaining fast, reliable audits, the profession finds that the audit itself has been marginalized in mainstream business.

Obviously this work will never go away—bookkeeping records, being the permanent archive of a company's actions, will always need to be certified as accurate by an outside, objective source. Nevertheless, like disk memory to the world of computer hardware and software, it remains fundamental but peripheral to the sweep of history.

For that reason, the big accounting firms have been casting about for new roles to play in corporate life. They have embarked on management consulting, the implementation of corporate information systems, even HR advice. It might be said that the big firms recognize they have a body of intellectual capital (accounting skills, electronic tools, strong customer relationships, a reputation for accuracy, honesty, and reliability) and are desperately searching for the best way to invest it.

Enter Intellectual Capital. And for the first time, the accounting profession is presented with a vast new opportunity that would appear to be a perfect fit to its talents. Being new and unproven, IC measurement is certain to contain flaws that we have not yet identified. Some of the current measurements may over time prove useless in determining value. By the same token, some critical new indices and indicators may still need to be discovered. This would be the perfect challenge for the accounting profession. It would be in the unique position (at least unique in the last half millennium) of being there at the founding of new business measurement system and being able to establish the rules and standards that it will have to follow.

At the same time, the very novelty of Intellectual Capital measurement suggests that we have little idea yet how clever minds may abuse it. The accounting audit process itself, beginning with the first such audit of Great Western Railroad more than a century ago, was devised to head off the unexpected abuses of traditional accounting by inserting an objective arbiter that would certify the propriety (if not the accuracy) of the accounting process. IC reporting, being still relatively inchoate, the creature of fast-moving processes and largely subjective data, is likely to prove even more vulnerable to misuse.

All of this suggests four important new roles for accounting firms:

1. *Design.* To use their new skill at systems design to help companies set up cost-effective, accurate IC monitoring programs and databases.
2. *Standards.* To monitor the development of Intellectual Capital reporting, determining which metrics do predict ultimate value and which do not, establish presentational formats in the new media, benchmark, and help government regulators establish case law and precedent for the punishment of violations.
3. *Certification.* Establish a methodology for conducting, validating, and certifying corporate Intellectual Capital audits.
4. *Navigation.* Assist in the search for patterns of value creation.

This is a huge opportunity for the accounting industry to get back in the middle of the action. Yet there are two obvious obstacles to the profession doing so.

The first is philosophical. Traditional financial accounting is a retrospective, definitive process: Here is precisely what happened financially during this period of the past. Intellectual Capital reporting, especially in the years to come, will be more immediate and indefinite. Can the accounting industry make this cognitive shift? Sveiby for one is doubtful, arguing that for a profession to relearn itself is an almost insurmountable challenge. On the other hand, the very fact that these firms have expanded into new markets such as corporate information systems suggests there may be hope.

The second obstacle is legal. Attend a Big Six conference these days and you're likely to get an earful about the fundamental paradox facing the profession: How do you build the kind of close, trusting relationship with your clients that the new business model demands, while at the same time fulfilling the legal requirement of maintaining an objective distance?

There is no easy answer to this question. Keep accounting firms at arm's length from their clients and they will not only become even more irrelevant but nowadays lose much of their business. Let them get too close and the objectivity that is the very foundation of the profession may become suspect.

The answer the profession is slowly groping toward appears to be that of "objectivity with proximity"—a relationship accepted by the clients because it is to their advantage to have validated financial reporting, and made possible for the accounting firms through even more stringent controls and more accurate (and repeatable) measurable tools . . . ironically, in itself an illustration of the creation of Intellectual Capital through collaboration with clients.

It sounds good in theory, but the efforts of the accounting industry to get to that goal could be waylaid at any moment by the SEC, by a crusading congressman or senator, or simply by one glaring case of abuse.

Should that happen, and the accounting profession be stymied in its attempt to take on the work of Intellectual Capital reporting, no doubt some other profession—probably the big consulting firms that have, in many cases, spun out of accounting—will step in to take on the job. But that will be a loss to almost everyone else: IC reporting will lose precious standardization time because it will lack the imprimatur of certified measurement, companies will continue to be misvalued, and most of all, the accounting profession will have missed the first big opportunity for professional renewal and development into the new century.

11

A Common Value

With the construction of an Intellectual Capital report we would seem to have completed our mission. But, in fact, we've just begun.

Intellectual Capital measurement is a revolutionary idea—and like most revolutions, it will refuse to stay within the bounds set for it. The Industrial Revolution didn't stop with the water-powered loom but went on to revise the arts, sciences, business, government, the very organization of society, and, ultimately, even the way people thought. So, too, with the so-called Second Industrial Revolution of the 1870s, which created not just the modern factory but hierarchical business and the bureaucratic society.

Today we are experiencing the same sweeping changes with the Information Revolution. The radical discontinuity wrought by the semiconductor integrated circuit, especially the microprocessor, is sending a shock wave outward to every corner of modern life.

Yet, history has shown that during these revolutionary periods, the participants are perpetually convinced that the latest change will be the last. That the sole application of this new technology will be to improve existing processes; and that, fundamentally, the way things are done will not appreciably change beyond becoming faster, cheaper, or more efficient.

History also teaches us that these predictions are *always* wrong, that the real impact comes in ways that no one fully expected, that even the definition of what is important changes forever. Thus, the telephone didn't replace the telegraph; instead, it created a whole new society based on communication. Television wasn't radio with pictures, but the heart of a new social order. And mass production didn't just make manufactured goods at less expense, but redefined the relationship between man and the natural world.

The measurement of Intellectual Capital may not be as earth-shaking as these others . . . but then again it just might. After all, when you change what you value you ultimately change your goals and reorient your strategies for getting there. For now, however, what all of this implies is beyond our imaginations, and certainly beyond the purview of this book—except to say that general acceptance of Intellectual Capital will certainly change the way businesses are organized and managed, as well as redirect the flow of investment in the world economy. For now, that's awesome enough.

In the meantime, what we can say with absolute certainty is that IC measurement, like other revolutions, will refuse to be constrained by precedent, and will create new, higher levels of linkages and synthesis than have heretofore been possible.

In particular, by focusing upon processes rather than financial results, IC measurement vaults the traditional chasm between for-profit and nonprofit institutions. This is an astounding change, whose implications grow larger the more you reflect upon them: because it means, for the first time in history, we can *compare the value of all institutions in society.*

The precise reader may have already noticed—and been annoyed by the fact—that throughout this book we have been rather loose with the words "firm," "company," "organization" "enterprise," and "institution," treating them as if they were interchangeable. Now we can admit we did that on purpose. In contemporary usage, those terms are not strictly interchangeable, but more like nested within another—that is, all companies are organizations but not visa versa.

But now look again at the metrics of the Intellectual Capital Annual Report in the last chapter. Notice how nearly all of them could be applied just as easily to the Boy Scouts of America or the International Red Cross as IBM and Mercedes-Benz. On one hand, this shouldn't be too surprising; after all, every organization shares certain common characteristics, including management, a decision-making structure, skilled employees, and an audience/market/constituency that influences its decisions.

Moreover, once one pulls away from the long-term financial structure, with its critical distinctions between for profit, not for profit, and nonprofit, and turns instead to the day-to-day life of the operation, every organization looks pretty much alike. There are issues of employee training and productivity, history and custom, management decision making, contractors to pay, and networks of alliances. Clothing aside, the events of a typical day in a typical office of the United States Army are not that much different from the same activities at Cambridge University or Deutschebank.

On the other hand, it is utterly amazing to contemplate the possibility of finding a universal yardstick for comparing value creation at all of these diverse institutions. Suddenly you *can* compare apples and oranges—not by looking at the fruit, but at the trees—especially the roots—from which they come.

But how? The Skandia story provides a clue. Remember how we took the Skandia indicators and indices, designed for a financial institution, and transferred most of them—some directly, some by translating to more universal terms, some by converting their underlying theme into a more widely used form—to our general IC report format? Then why not do it again to achieve an even higher level of commonality?

We have no doubt that if, say, Microsoft, Intel, the U.S. Department of Commerce, and Yale University were to prepare their own IC reports, they would each be forced to change some of the indices of the standard format, as well as add a few new ones unique to their field. For example, Microsoft, as a software company, would want to exhibit metrics that reflect the absolutely central role played in its industry by standardization. Software companies will spend tens, even hundreds, of millions of dollars giving away software in order to capture the position of industry standard, as Microsoft's Windows 95 does today. Owning such a standard offers a huge, sometimes insurmountable, advantage over the competition and can all but guarantee years of stronger revenues and growing profitability.

As Eric Schmidt, chief technology officer for Sun Microsystems Inc., a computer workstation maker that has done just such a standard-creating giveaway with its Java software, told *The Wall Street Journal,* "There's no GDP gained in giving the product away and yet it can create enormous value by building up a franchise." Schmidt calls this technique, "Ubiquity now, revenue later."[1]

Traditional bookkeeping at best doesn't account for this standard building, and at worst punishes it. The Intellectual Capital model shows it in the proper light. Even more so if a company like Microsoft or Sun chooses to highlight this program with added indices and indicators related to customer base penetration, applications program designers signed on to develop for that operating system, and the like.

Similarly, Intel would want to display its advantages in owning the dominant architecture in microprocessors, the so-called x86, and it would want to count the number of "design-wins" this architecture has among personal-computer and video-game makers. But just as important, Intel has a tremendous Intellectual Capital asset in its "Intel Inside" branding campaign, which recent global surveys credit with customer recognition on the level of Coca-Cola or Disney. Intel would surely want a "brand recognition" or "share of mind" measure.

The Intellectual Capital of the Commerce Department, by comparison, lies in its expertise at stopping illegal importations and in its ability to negotiate new business contracts for U.S. corporations. The agency would want to measure and display each of these value-creating perspectives, probably related to the number and value of interdictions and to the number and value of new international business contracts.

Yale University's Intellectual Capital would seem to lie almost exclusively in the brains of its professoriate, but in fact its structural capital may be even more important. One might begin by counting the advanced degrees owned by Yale's professors, but it would quickly be apparent that this wouldn't be enough to distinguish the unique strengths of Yale over those, say, of a suburban state college in California, which might have more total Ph.D.'s. Measurements of honorary degrees, however, might help, as might publication rates, graduation rates of doctoral students, average salary growth of new graduates, name recognition, an index of desirability by graduating high school students, research networks, and so forth.

However, even these would not be enough to capture the true value and influence of an Ivy League university that continues to develop some of the most important thinkers and leaders in America, including U.S. presidents, as well as many of its most respected actors and actresses. For that, the university would likely need to survey its graduates on a regular basis to establish their roles in government, industry, and the arts and measure the amount of their regular contacts with the daily life of the university. Such measures, along with others designed to gauge the Ivy League network and its role in the governance, the culture, and the economy of the United States, would give some clue to the true value of Yale.

DETERMINING THE IC EQUATION

Having begun by talking about the commonalities possible with the Intellectual Capital model, we seem to have instead been listing the differences. But keep in mind, all of these diverse and specialized measures are merely *distinctions* above and beyond the core body of common IC indices. At its heart, the IC model does seem to hold for all different kinds of enterprises.

What these distinctions do show is that it is probably impossible to come up with a truly universal IC reporting model that will fit everyone. Rather, the model constructed in the last chapter is precisely that: a model from which institutions and business can work to create a format that best fits them.

This isn't earthshaking news. After all, the current financial accounting pages vary company by company and industry by industry. Still, to come so close to a universal measurement system for all organizations and stop because it isn't a perfect fit would be a terrible loss.

So, let's revisit the problem. First, keep in mind that we currently have a way of comparing the financial performance between two for-profit companies: It consists of revenues, profits, and earnings per share. Only the last is a precisely defined figure. By comparison, the definition of revenues and profits are more fluid, often requiring additional information ("profits included a one-time write-off for losses relating to the recall of defective Pentium chips") for the sake of accuracy and investor comprehension. This suggests that any universal IC yardstick will also allow for a degree of inexactness, as long as we know, and express, what and where those limitations are. It is better to be roughly right than precisely wrong.

Second, we also know that, because we are dealing with the present and the future, not the past, internal and external factors may come into play to affect any value computation we do.

Third, and maybe most important, we intuitively sense that, because it deals with behavior, talents, organization, and value-producing property, our IC yardstick, in some form, can be applied to any organization.

These three principles seem to suggest that:

1. If we can find a core of indices in our IC model that can, with minimum translation, be applied across society;

2. If we can ratify this core group, while recognizing that each organization may have additional Intellectual Capital that must be measured by other indices; and,
3. If can establish some variable that captures the less-than-perfect predictability of the future as well as the less-than-perfect behavior of equipment, organizations, and people in an organization;

then we can find our universal comparison.

What we are looking for then is something like this:

Organizational Intellectual Capital = i C

where C is some value of Intellectual Capital in dollars and i is that organization's *coefficient of efficiency* in using that Intellectual Capital.

MEASURING THE IC EQUATION

The challenge now is determining how to compute these two figures.

Look again at our standard model:

The Intellectual Capital Report

FINANCIAL FOCUS
1. Total assets ($)
2. Total assets/employee ($)
3. Revenues/total assets (%)
4. Profits/total assets ($)
5. Revenues resulting from new business operations ($)
6. Profits resulting from new business operations ($)
7. Revenues/employee ($)

8. Customer time/employee attendance (%)
9. Profits/employee ($)
10. Lost business revenues compared to market average (%)
11. Revenues from new customers/total revenues (%)
12. Market value ($)
13. Return on net asset value (%)
14. Return on net assets resulting from new business operations ($)
15. Value added/employee ($)
16. Value added/IT-employees ($)
17. Investments in IT ($)
18. Value added/customer ($)

CUSTOMER FOCUS
1. Market share (%)
2. Number of customers (#)
3. Annual sales/customer ($)
4. Customers lost (#)
5. Average duration of customer relationship (#)
6. Average customer size ($)
7. Customer rating (%)
8. Customer visits to the company (#)
9. Days spent visiting customers (#)
10. Customers/employees ($)
11. Field salespeople (#)
12. Field sales management (#)
13. Average time from customer contact to sales response (#)
14. Ratio of sales contacts to sales closed (%)
15. Satisfied Customer Index (%)
16. IT investment/salesperson ($)
17. IT investment/service and support employee ($)
18. Support expense/customer ($)
19. Service expense/customer/year ($)
20. Service expense/customer/contact ($)

Process Focus

1. Administrative expense/total revenues (#)
2. Cost for administrative error/management revenues (%)
3. Processing time, outpayments (#)
4. Contracts filed without error (#)
5. Function points/employee-month (#)
6. PCs/employee (#)
7. Laptops/employee (#)
8. Administrative expense/employee ($)
9. IT expense/employee ($)
10. IT expense/administrative expense (%)
11. Administrative expense/gross premium (%)
12. IT capacity (CPU and DASD) (#)
13. Change in IT inventory ($)
14. Corporate quality goal (#)
15. Corporate performance/quality goal (%)
16. Discontinued IT inventory/IT inventory (%)
17. Orphan IT inventory/IT inventory (%)
18. IT capacity/employee (#)
19. IT performance/employee (#)

Renewal and Development Focus

1. Competence development expense/employee ($)
2. Satisfied Employee Index (#)
3. Marketing expense/customer ($)
4. Share of training hours (%)
5. Share of development hours (%)
6. Opportunity share (%)
7. R&D expense/administrative expense (%)
8. Training expense/employee ($)
9. Training expense/administrative expense (%)
10. Business development expense/administrative expense (%)
11. Share of employees below age 40 (%)
12. IT development expense/IT expense (%)

13. IT expenses on training/IT expense (%)
14. R&D resources/total resources (%)
15. Customer opportunity base captured (#)
16. Average customer age (#)
    education (#)
    income (#)
17. Average customer duration with company in months (#)
18. Educational investment/customer ($)
19. Direct communications to customer/year (#)
20. Non-product-related expense/customer/year ($)
21. New markets development investment ($)
22. Structural capital development investment ($)
23. Value of EDI system ($)
24. Upgrades to EDI system ($)
25. Capacity of EDI system (#)
26. Ratio of new products (less than two years) to full company product family (%)
27. R&D invested in basic research (%)
28. R&D invested in product design (%)
29. R&D invested in applications (%)
30. Investment in new product support and training ($)
31. Average age of company patents (#)
32. Patents pending (#)

HUMAN FOCUS
1. Leadership Index (%)
2. Motivation Index (%)
3. Empowerment Index (#)
4. Number of employees (#)
5. Employee turnover (%)
6. Average years of service with company (#)
7. Number of managers (#)
8. Number of women managers (#)
9. Average age of employees (#)
10. Time in training (days/year) (#)

11. IT-literacy of staff (#)
12. Number of full-time/permanent employees (#)
13. Average age of full-time/permanent employees (#)
14. Average years with company of full-time permanent employees (#)
15. Annual turnover of full-time permanent employees (#)
16. Per capita annual cost of training, communication, and support programs for full-time permanent employees ($)
17. Full-time/permanent employees who spend less than 50 percent of work hours at a corporate facility
    Percentage of full-time permanent employees
    Per capita annual cost of training, communication, and support programs
18. Number of full-time temporary employees
    Average years with company of full-time temporary employees
19. Per capita annual cost of training and support programs for full-time temporary employees ($)
20. Number of part-time employees/non-full-time contractors (#)
21. Average duration of contract (#)
23. Percentage of company managers with advanced degrees
    Business (%)
    Advanced science and engineering degrees (%)
    Advanced liberal arts degrees (%)

Notice that there are actually three different types of measurements: direct counts, dollar amounts, and percentages. If we assume that the direct counts (#) are essentially raw or unprocessed data destined to either be compared to other direct counts to produce a ratio (%) or to be transformed into money ($), then we are really looking at just two types of measurements.

It follows neatly that the monetary measures, our indicators, in some way combine to produce an Intellectual Capital value (C) for the organization. Meanwhile, the percentages, our indices, which after all are a measure of incompleteness, in some way combine to produce the coefficient of Intellectual Capital efficiency by capturing the organization's velocity, position, and direction.

MEASURING IC VALUE

Let's begin with C, the value of an organization's Intellectual Capital. Call it the absolute measure, as it is the core value we will work from. What indicators do we sum to achieve a realistic and comparable figure?

It seems practical to start with the Navigator, which implicitly suggests that whatever indicators we choose, they must be representative of each of the five focuses. If we do that, cross-referencing each focus by the monetary measures they contain, we come up with thirty-six indicators. However, many of them are themselves ratios (for example, "value added/employee"), so we must multiply out the denominators.

Now, we remove any redundancies, as well as any entries ("total assets") that properly belong on the balance sheet, and we end up with about two dozen indices—a number that about equals the approximately twenty indices Skandia found to be a manageable amount for easy measurement and computation.

You might wish to try the same exercise. If you do, you will likely agree with us that while this gets us close to a workable value, there are still some factors missing that can only be added through judgment calls.

Here is our list:

Intellectual Capital Absolute Measure (C) Indicators

(All measurements for fiscal year)

1. Revenues resulting from new business operations (new programs/services)

2. New markets (customer/client/curriculum) development investment
3. Industry development investment
4. New channel development investment
5. IT investment in sales, service, and support
6. IT investment in administration
7. Change in IT inventory
8. Customer (client) support investment
9. Customer (client) service investment
10. Customer (client) training investment
11. Non-product-related customer expense
12. Employee competence development investment
13. Employee new product support and training investment
14. Education unique to non-company-based employees
15. Training, communication, and support investment unique to full-time permanent employees
16. Training and support programs unique to full-time temporary employees
17. Training and support programs unique to part-time temporary employees
18. Partnership/joint venture development investment
19. Upgrades to EDI or electronic networking system
20. Brand (logo/name) identification investment
21. New patent, copyright investment

Note that this list consists of topical clusters. For example, the first group (1–4) emphasizes new business development, the second (5–7) IT investment, then customer development (8–11), employee development (12–17), partnerships (18–19), and finally branding and intellectual property (20–21).

Is this a definitive list? Hardly. It is only designed to start the debate on what does constitute Intellectual Capital value. Moreover, our list, by looking at investment, only emphasizes future earnings capabilities. But Intellectual Capital also involves current capabilities, and for that a different list might be created that looks only at estimated value for such things as existing patents, training programs, and customer demand. We chose the former because we think it captures more of what investors need to know about the future value of a company. We also think that a current value measurement system would be both very difficult to do and ripe for mismeasurement, overoptimism (after all, what is the current value of a patent that has yet to be made into a product?), and even fraud. In particular, it fails the Davidow Test: That is, it would allow a company to make extravagant claims for a product or service that as yet has no record of success.

So, investment in the future is the key. But we are still only halfway there. A bad or misdirected investment is usually worse than none at all. So the next step is to create a countervailing figure that tests these investments against real-life productivity, value creation, and user evaluation.

A COEFFICIENT OF EFFICIENCY

The coefficient of Intellectual Capital efficiency (i) is the truth detector of our equation. As the absolute (C) variable emphasizes an organization's commitment to the future, the efficiency (i) variable grounds those claims in present performance.

Let's return to the general report and this time extract only the percentages and ratios, the indices, then once more cull out redundancies and apply some subjective judgments:

Intellectual Capital Coefficient of Efficiency (i) Indices

(All measurements current)

1. Market share (%)
2. Satisfied Customer Index (%)
3. Leadership Index (%)

4. Motivation Index (%)
5. Index of R&D resources/total resources (%)
6. Index of training hours (%)
7. Performance/quality goal (%)
8. Employee retention (%)
9. Administrative efficiency/revenues (reciprocal of administrative error/revenues) (%)

Notice, first of all, that there are fewer indices here, but those that remain are more sweeping in their scope. Also, once again, the choice of indices is designed to reflect the structure of the Navigator—only this time we are looking for current measures of the success (or failure) of the focuses. Moreover, when possible, we use external, objective analysis of these factors rather than the company's own, inevitably self-serving, claims.

We should also note that, unlike the Leadership and Motivation Indexes as they were computed for Skandia, for our purposes they must be converted into percentages so as to have the same form for all nine indices.

Now, all of that said, somehow this group of nine indices might be combined into a single percentage that will accurately reflect how effectively the organization is currently using its Intellectual Capital. To do that, each must increase in value the better the company performs. So, items like "employee turnover" must be reversed to "employee retention," and "administrative error costs/revenues" needs to become "administrative efficiency/revenues." Others, such as R&D investment and training hours, need to indexed against the industry average.

Here then is our suggested equation:

$$i = (n/x)$$

where (n) equals the sum of the decimal values for the nine efficiency indices and (x) the number of those indices. In other words, determine the average of the indices.

As an example, consider an organization with the following efficiency index values:

1. Market share (%) = .46
2. Satisfied Customer Index (%) = .78
3. Leadership Index (%) = .45
4. Motivation Index (%) = .53
5. R&D Resources Index (%) = .93
6. Training Hours Index (%) = .95
7. Performance/quality goal (%) = .91
8. Employee retention (%) = .87
9. Administrative efficiency/revenues (%) = .91

This would yield an efficiency coefficient of i = 85%.

Were the company to have IC absolute measure of, say, $200 million, this would result in an overall common IC measure for the company of:

$$i\,C = .85(\$200 \text{ million})$$

$$= \$170 \text{ million}$$

You can see that while a complete breakdown in one part of a organization's operations would have a damaging effect on its Intellectual Capital valuation, it would at most diminish the coefficient by just over 12 percent—a figure that seems reasonable in the real world of business. Conversely, it would be virtually impossible for any company to achieve a coefficient greater than 1, such that it would actually increase its absolute measure. Yet, it also seems reasonable that if a company were to do so, it would be such a competitive powerhouse that it would indeed be amplifying its value, and would deserve such a rare distinction.

IC AND M & A

Before we even look at formal applications for this common measure, one obvious application that requires no regulation is in mergers and acquisitions. Here the common measure, and the metrics that form it, can be immediately put to use in comparing firms and determining if they truly represent a viable fit.

This can be done in levels of detail, beginning with the common measure. A wide divergence here is a danger signal that there are fundamental structural differences between two organizations.

The nature of these differences is likely to be exposed by looking at the indicators in the absolute measure, and even more so by the indices of the efficiency coefficient. Here, problems can be identified and then traced back to the even more specific IC report, even to the appendix of other measures.

At this point it may become apparent that the problem is a deal-breaker. Or it might prove fixable, and in that case might be the basis for a more accurate valuation. In either case, the companies participating enter into negotiations with a better knowledge of the other than ever before, and the resulting deal (or nondeal) will be more economically valid and efficient than traditional mergers and acquisitions based only on product lines, company reputation, or balance sheets.

Given the number of mergers and acquisitions that occur each year that result in companies that are either crippled by debt or tearing themselves to pieces because of incompatible corporate cultures, having such a new evaluation tool is no small matter.

THE INTELLECTUAL CAPITAL OF MUNICIPALITIES

Let's take a closer look at how Intellectual Capital measurement can be a useful tool for evaluating a noncommercial institution. Consider the valuation of cities and towns.

Predicting the future is always a risky business, but one can say with a certain amount of assurance that the twenty-first century will see radical changes in where and how people live. In particular, the combination of powerful communications technologies with equally powerful information technologies will make it possible for people to live and work nearly anywhere and still enjoy most of the fruits of life in a big city or suburbia or the countryside—from culture and the arts to role-playing and simulated participation in distant world events.

These same technologies will also make work more and more portable, shifting jobs from centralized work sites (office buildings and factories) to virtual offices located at home or on the road or in neighborhood centers.

Most of this is already known to the reader, who may already be feeling the pull of this approaching future. And in each of us there is forming a question that will likely be the defining one of the next century:

If we can live and work anywhere, where shall we live and work?

This is a kind of freedom that mankind has rarely ever known in its history. Now it may well be the lifestyle of a majority of the population.

But, in one of life's bigger ironies, freedom always brings with it new responsibilities. Faced with this infinite choice of how and where to live and work, what will we choose? Will everyone race to the cities, or to the countryside? Will mountain and seaside resorts suddenly swell with new year-round residents? Will small towns suddenly see a burst of growth as prodigal grandsons and granddaughters return to their ancestral homes in search of family and security? Or will people take to the road as cybergypsies, linked to a distant home base only by their technological umbilicals?

Whatever choices are made, they will inevitably transform the dynamic of municipalities, creating new challenges and amplifying competition.

We have been down this road before.[2] In the years before the Civil War, the factory towns of the northeastern United States were the envy of the world. These towns, such as Elizabeth and Paterson, New Jersey, and Manchester, New Hampshire, had found the right combination of both physical and intellectual capital—technology (looms), power (waterwheels), employees (northern European immigrants), infrastructure (interchangeable parts), and transportation (canals)—to become wealthy and powerful. The business leaders of these towns saw to it that their towns—now cities—remained state of the art. Paterson was even designed from scratch in 1797 by a consortium led by Alexander Hamilton to use the nearby Passaic River to power an ideal new factory city.

These cities were adaptable too. Beginning in the 1840s, Paterson and Lowell, Massachusetts, even converted their own older textile mills and became the nation's leading manufacturers of locomotives. By the Civil War and its boom in demand for manufactured goods, these cities were ready for the call . . . and indeed, history records that the mill towns of the Northeast powered the Union victory.

After the war, there was every reason to believe that these now rich communities, with their giant factories and new mansions, museums, universities, and libraries, would remain the dynamo of the U.S. economy. All they needed was to remain vigilant, upgrade their facilities, and implement new technologies—the recipe for success that had kept them on top for nearly a century.

But it didn't happen. Talent (intellectual capital) moved elsewhere; so did money (financial capital). By 1901, when Pittsburgh-based U.S. Steel became the first billion-dollar, 100,000 employee company, three hundred firms in the United States were capitalized at more than $10 million . . . and almost none of them were in the old mill towns.

Where were they? In towns like Chicago and St. Louis, Pittsburgh and Detroit, where new factories were run by new technologies (steam and electricity), using new forms of transportation (railroads and, eventually, trucking), new types of labor (eastern European immigrants), and a different infrastructure (mass production, bureaucracies).

Why did the northeastern mill towns fail? Not from stupidity or obsolescence, nor even lassitude. They failed not because they wavered from their recipe for success but because they stuck to it while the rest of the world changed.

For nearly a century now, the towns and cities of the industrial world have lived that new municipal paradigm to varying degrees of success. The modern city, if it plans at all, tries for a balance between large companies and small, manufacturers and service providers, a range of housing, and sufficient postsecondary education to keep the best and brightest children home. What character these towns and cities have is typically the result of fortune, geography, and sometimes a strong or famous resident. The model has worked because it has been the best fit for the twentieth-century reality of television, the automobile, universal mass production, and mass marketing.

But now the equation is again being recast, the balance of forces reset. We sense that the new mix will again combine new technologies (microprocessor-based products), transportation (the Internet and broadband telecommunications), labor (the mix of office goers, telecommuters, road warriors, and corporate gypsies), and infrastructure (virtual organizations). City planners also suggest that this extraordinary new level of choice in being able to live anywhere will create a panoramic self-sorting of the population into cities and towns as theme parks, by which each municipality will stress certain characteristics that match the lifestyles of targeted populations—young parents, professionals, senior citizens, cocooners, urban young people, and so on.

Combine all of these factors and once more we see the familiar outlines of the IC Navigator, with its mix of the human factor (citizens), customers (the businesses that support or employ these citizens, as well as those being recruited to come to town), and process (the municipality's mix of city government, schools, police, fire department, and so forth). There is also, of course, the financial factor, which combines the city's budget (including debt or surplus), tax base, and the combined local investment of the area's businesses.

Tellingly, what is all but missing in most municipalities is the renewal and development factor. This is due less to the fact that cities and towns don't fit the IC Navigator than that, complacent after a century of predictable change, they have allowed programs to develop these indirect assets to atrophy. That hasn't been a bad strategy in the past, but as with the New England mill towns of the 1870s, it may be a suicidal strategy for the future. Even for the present: The growing voter frustration in the United States with government inefficiency, from the federal bureaucracy down to the local city government—and the call by the Clinton administration, among others, for "reinventing government"— would seem to reflect a growing frustration with established models and traditional ways to measure their efficiency and value creation.

If the Navigator works with municipalities, then it follows that comparable indictors and indices can be translated over as well.

Do they? Look, for example, at the Process Focus in our universal IC reporting format and let's try to translate it to a city government:

PROCESS FOCUS
1. Administrative expense/total revenues (#)
2. Cost for administrative error/management revenues (%)
3. Processing time, permits (#)
4. Permits filed without error (#)
5. Average response time, police and fire department (#)
6. Felonies per capita/annual (#)

   • Murder (#)
   • Rape (#)
   • Drug abuse (#)

- Burglary (#)
- Assault (#)

7. Function points/employee-month (#)
8. PCs/employee (#)
9. Laptops/employee (#)
10. Average IT access speed per capita (#)
11. Annual investment in new parks and recreation facilities ($)
12. Administrative expense/employee ($)
13. IT expense/employee ($)
14. Emergency response program investment
15. Average annual educational expense per
     elementary student
     secondary student
16. Return (test scores) on educational investment
     elementary
     secondary
17. Annual hours of postsecondary education per capita (older than 18)
18. Average annual infrastructure investment per capita
19. IT expense/administrative expense (%)
20. Administrative expense per dollar of tax revenue (%)
21. IT capacity (CPU and DASD) (#)
22. Change in IT inventory ($)
23. Municipal quality goal (#)
24. Municipal performance/quality goal (%)
25. Discontinued IT inventory/IT inventory (%)
26. Orphan IT inventory/IT inventory (%)
27. IT capacity/employee (#)
28. IT performance/employee (#)
29. Average ambulance response time (#)
30. Average ambulance delivery to hospital time (#)
31. Number of hospital beds within twenty miles (#)
32. Combined rating of medical facilities within twenty miles (%)

33. Average commute time to nearest domestic airline (#)
34. Average commute time to nearest international airline (#)
35. Average commute time by citizens to work (#)
36. Average annual smog index (#)
37. Average air alert days per year (#)

Obviously this could be refined even more, with additional indicators rewritten and others added, but for now the point seems clear that such a translation can be made.

Thus far in this application, the Navigator would seem to be merely a more sophisticated form of the annual surveys done by magazines such as *Fortune* for the best cities to live in—the crucial difference being that the indicators in this model are more aligned to what the municipality is becoming rather than what it currently is (and in the case of the Financial Focus, where it has just been).

Nowhere would this be more the case than in the Renewal and Development Focus. Needless to say, the indicators in that focus must be very carefully defined so as to capture a society in flux, pointing the way toward currently unimaginable new forms rather than merely measuring the currently received view of the future.

The next question, obviously, is: Can we continue this process? In particular, what we need are indices that:

1. Elaborate upon the fundamental question—If you could live anywhere would you live here?—referencing it to different economic and demographic groups (age, profession, type of worker, and so forth).

2. Compare those responses with the municipality's own goals for the economic and demographic mix of its citizenry. (For example, is the city trying to be a mecca for young white-collar parents when it is blue-collar senior citizens who want to stay?)

3. Correlate the targeted renewal and development invest-

ments made by the community with the results from numbers 1 and 2 (for example, should the city be building more elementary schools or senior centers?).

4. Measure the investments being made by the municipality to either shift its future toward the new goal or shift away from that goal back to a model more congruent with its present.

5. Combine all of these factors to determine not just the Intellectual Capital of the municipality but the efficiency (and risk) of its use of this capital. Thus, the community that is investigating in a manner at odds with its current reality or future goals is obviously working at a lesser efficiency than one in harmony with its present and future.

We've already made a pass at just such indicators for the Process Focus. It is outside the scope of this book (and the authors' expertise) to prepare a complete and standardized IC report for municipalities—that would be a useful project for the U.S. Chamber of Commerce or for a professional organization such as the National Council of Mayors. For our purposes, it seems reasonable to assume that such a report can be prepared and that in time will be made even more accurate a measure of the indirect assets of municipalities.

Now, if we have all these measurements, as well as a Navigator, can we make the final step and use our two-variable IC measure, i C, for municipalities? Probably. Look again at those five requirements we have for our municipal IC indices—aren't they precisely what we are looking for to determine the coefficient of efficiency in that measure?

All of this suggests that if we can begin the process of IC measurement for municipalities—that is, establish metrics—we can do all of the rest, from IC reporting to simple comparative measures. And if we can do that for towns and cities, then it also seems to follow that we can do it for almost every other institution of any kind—and thus universally assert a new, more balanced perspective on wealth and its creation.

A HISTORY LESSON

With that we reach the culmination of the process that began with frustration over the inadequacy of traditional accounting to capture the dynamic and intangible nature of modern business value creation.

We now have a navigational technique to serve as the organizer for our new measurement system. A body of nearly one hundred measurements in five categories to capture and present this data. And finally, a mechanism for summarizing this body of information into a single encompassing measure that allows for the comparison of value between not only diverse business enterprises but seemingly every kind of human organization.

When Columbus embarked upon the greatest adventure of his era, he sailed handicapped by a flawed measurement system. Whereas he could readily determine the latitude of his small fleet quite accurately, he had only limited means by which to establish longitude. That he reached San Salvador island in the Americas rather than his goal of India was a bit of luck even he never quite believed.

Ultimately, the measurement of longitude had to wait upon the development of a new technology—precise chronometers that could remain accurate to within a few minutes per year—and the new perspective that arose from it. Though these chronometers were generally available to seafarers by the end of the eighteenth century, it would still take another century, until 1884, before the nations of the world agreed upon a common standard for that measurement: Greenwich Mean Time.

Drawing analogies to Columbus and the Age of Exploration has become something of a cliché. Nevertheless, in light of our subject, certain comparisons seem clear: Information technology is the great adventure of our time, one that is changing every part of our lives. Yet we are applying this technology, building millions of new institutions, revamping our system of rewards and punishments, ultimately resting our economy upon navigational tools that are obviously obsolete and misguiding.

Now, at last, an answer has appeared—a new navigational system that offers a more precise measure of where we are and where we are going. Will it take a century for us to adopt it as a common standard?

12

A Future Market

A new measure of value always establishes an exchange system to trade that value.

In the Middle Ages, the trade was barter exchange or monetary. You brought the crops you grew or the livestock you husbanded or the crafts you produced to the nearest market town, where you either exchanged those items, via barter, for other items you perceived of at least comparable worth. Or, you were paid in gold, which in turn enabled you to purchase other goods.

Even in this basic market economy it was sometimes possible to lend money at interest. And this debt could be sold at discount from one lender to another, thus creating an exchange in debts.

A few hundred years later, the exchange process had been streamlined by taking the transaction process one step removed: that is, by the widespread use of money, which served as a guaranteed, convertible surrogate for gold. With the return of the widespread use of coinage (it having been largely out of general circulation since the Roman era), and the first-ever use of paper money, another layer of exchange was created—that of capital stock. The first such stock exchange was opened in Amsterdam in the seventeenth century.

With the passage of another century, the exchange process had become specialized. For example, in the 1750s it was possible to walk by the coffeehouses that lined "Change Alley" in London and watch speculators buying and selling shares inside the particular coffeehouse that specialized in their industry. Thus, Edward Lloyd's coffeehouse specialized in maritime insurance; Casey's in fire insurance—and from that humble start both would create giant firms that survive today.[1] In the words of the French historian of everyday life, Ferdinand Braudel, Change Alley became "the rendezvous of those who, having money already, wished to own more, as well as of the more numerous class of men, who having nothing, hoped to attract the money of those who possessed it."[2]

The arrival of the Industrial Revolution took the process to yet another level. By the end of the nineteenth century, at exchanges throughout the world, but especially on Wall Street in New York, brokers were buying and selling millions of shares of corporate stock each day in a frenzy of speculation that forever changed the nature of capital formation. A thousand miles away in Chicago the Board of Exchange, thanks to the information revolution wrought by the telegraph, telephone, and railroad, was converting itself from a commodity exchange to a commodity *futures* exchange, in which brokers began to speculate on information about corn and gold and pork bellies rather than on the items themselves.

By the turn of the twentieth century, the essential nature of capital and futures exchanges was largely in place; and so this century has been spent developing new investment tools and forms, as well as in expanding the base of investors. Thus, at the turn of the millennium, in the United States, more than 100 million private individuals own enough shares in stocks, options, mutual funds, and indices to make them the majority owners over institutional investors. And this is only part of a global phenomenon: Each day more than $1.5 *trillion* flows through the world's financial system—ten times more than in the so-called real industrial economy.

The last twenty-five years have also seen the creation of a new form, if not type, of exchange. NASDAQ specializes in volatile new technology-company stocks, and the exchange's structure matches that of its clients: Using massive computer databases and high-speed telecommunications, NASDAQ essentially is a virtual stock exchange, existing mostly in data alone without the traditional trading floor and brokering stations. NASDAQ points the way to the future.

Now we have a new measure of value, Intellectual Capital, as well as both a metric to evaluate it and a simple two-variable measure to compare it. Moreover, this new measure also has a larger subject base than any that have come before—encompassing not just commercial business but governmental and nonprofit institutions. It would seem inevitable that some new exchange system will arise to make use of this measure for speculative purposes.

THE BRADLEY-ALBERT MODEL

But what would such an Intellectual Capital Exchange look like? How would it operate? What would it trade? How would it be regulated?

The first attempt to imagine such an exchange was conducted in 1995 by Keith Bradley and Steven Albert of the London School of Economics Business Performance Group, a research institute that studies business performance.[3]

According to Bradley and Albert, the creation of such a "Knowledge Exchange" will be a natural progression from the commodity, capital, and financial exchanges that have preceded it. They also believe it highly unlikely that any of the traditional exchanges will be able to co-opt this process as an added service:

> These exchanges have problems in accurately valuing a company based on intellectual capital. Perhaps this is because these exchanges grew and matured and [have] been developing since the seventeenth century to exchange on paper (shares) backed by physical goods, like corn, wheat and automobiles. It is because of these long roots into the exchange of physical goods that these exchanges have developed a unique set of rules and customs which

govern their means of transaction. This might make them less efficient at coping with an invisible intellectual capital. [One reason
may be] that intellectual capital is not a commodity to be
exchanged, but a debt. . . . And yet it may be more fundamental
that this: stock markets appear to be less successful at valuing
intellectual capital because they are designed to perform a very different task.[4]

Given these problems, Bradley and Albert conclude that "we
must look elsewhere for the knowledge exchange."[5]

Their choice, perhaps due to Albert's expertise in employee
training and performance, is to look to the labor market as an
example of a protoknowledge exchange—in particular, the way
that specialized workers (managers, professionals, etc.) essentially
exchanges the future application of their talent, for the duration
of a contract, to the hiring company. Moreover, this type of
exchange is indeed a knowledge transaction, though Bradley and
Albert admit they see no immediate way to translate that transaction into a larger exchange system.

So they then look back at the history of other market
exchanges and note that in their infancy, each of these exchanges
began with specialists trading within a particular area of expertise, acting as speculators by "blank buying"—that is, selling
things they did not actually own and buying items they would
never actually possess. The growing expertise of these specialists
at bringing together far-flung buyers and sellers was the genesis
of the modern exchanges.

So, ask Bradley and Albert, is there any modern counterpart to
these streetside speculators in labor exchange?

As a matter of fact, there is. Temporary employment agencies
and large management consulting firms. These manpower agencies, Bradley and Albert write,

market experts' skills and knowledge through the placement of
professionals in various firms. Individuals' know-how or intellec-

tual capital is leased. The agent acts as a specialist and provides a venue for the leaseholder and lessor of knowledge.[6]

As with the rise of the capital and commodity exchanges, Bradley and Albert believe technological innovation will spur the expansion of these programs into vast, far-reaching enterprises. In particular, the rise of the Internet creates the perfect venue for global labor interchanges. Agencies will act as intermediaries "because the amount of information a potential lessor (employer) needs to digest is immense":

> For example, imagine there was a need for a computer programmer in Japan. If a company or group of individuals called up all computer programmers the searching for a match would take a lifetime. Some would be available, others not. Some would suit the tasks perfectly, other not at all. The search costs would be immense before the desired person could be found.
>
> Enter the specialist or agent. The agent's task would be to "edit" information and generate a list of the most suitable candidates for a specific potential employer. . . . It is this hiring of employees with their know-how that the agent excels at. And it is in the searching for and selection of the best exchange, or combination, that the agent provides an efficient market service to lubricate the knowledge economy.[7]

Bradley and Albert also believe this exchange works in the opposite direction, too. As with entertainment and sports, people would respond to demand by obtaining agents to represent and promote them to these global employment exchanges. In time, individuals with shared skills or talents would form organizations and networks, with precise membership requirements—sort of a jobs-oriented version of groups like the IEEE for electrical engineers and the AMA for doctors—to promote their interests, pool employment experience, and set hiring standards.

In the interplay between these two groups of representatives, employer and employee agents, all occurring lightning fast on the Internet, Bradley and Albert see an efficient means to allocate the intellectual resources of an economy.[8]

The Bradley-Albert model is compelling. And the choice of vehicle is inspired: The fact that executive and professional recruitment/placement agencies are among the hottest service industries in the world right now suggests that this industry is definitely answering some fundamental need in the economy. And there is no reason to believe that such a lucrative new business won't appear, with giant employment firms knitting together millions of individual skill sets, in the form of Web pages/résumés, according to the firm's own proprietary algorithms to produce the best fit with employer-customers.

Nevertheless, one can accept this model without accepting that it represents the true image of the new IC exchange. There are two reasons for our doubt:

1. *Employees are not all of Intellectual Capital.* Remember the Navigator. The brains and talents of human beings, the human capital, lie at the center of the IC model, but they are not all of the model. They may invent new products, but they are not the products themselves. They may read the results from corporate information systems, but they are not the computers. Nor are they the networking system or the organizational infrastructure. So, restricting the exchange of Intellectual Capital solely to the skills of workers is to miss a considerable portion of a company's IC value. Any exchange system must take these other leveraging factors also into account.

2. *True exchanges include speculation.* Bradley and Albert recognize this fact in describing the rise of commodities and capital exchanges, but then limit it when describing their Knowledge Exchange. Because of that, one must question whether what they describe is really an exchange at all; but rather, an emerging new service industry. Not a

small thing, certainly, but not the new IC stock market history suggests is coming. What we end up with in the Bradley-Albert model is certainly an exchange, but an exchange of *labor*, while the real goal is to find a different type of exchange—one of *values*.

The end result of the Bradley-Albert model would seem to be a comparatively small body of employment agencies and consultants managing a vast population of professional people, negotiating wages and fees and moving talent around the globe. Sure, this is a higher level of abstraction than the workers soliciting the jobs themselves, and yes, the employer is essentially buying a "future" on the work of the prospective professional. But there is little room in this scenario for the outside investor to choose among the many transactions and speculate on their change in value.

A TRUE IC EXCHANGE

But even if this is not the exchange model for IC, Bradley and Albert have both raised the possibility of such an exchange and pointed out some interesting characteristics of Intellectual Capital itself. These features, some suggested by their model and some in response to it, include:

1. Intellectual Capital is debt. That is, it is an investment in the futu_e whose ultimate return will eventually be determined.
2. Any IC exchange will be, by definition, a futures market, speculating on the nature of this return on investment.
3. This exchange must be open to third parties, not just intermediaries, who can speculate on the value of the anticipated return.
4. The structural nature of the exchange, such as the speed of

its transactions, must mirror the nature of Intellectual Capital itself.

So, what does this tell us about the true nature of an IC exchange? Once again, return to the Navigator. The message of its format is that Intellectual Capital is in fact a measurement system that tracks through time the flow of an organization's nontangible asset investments as they consolidate and successfully or unsuccessfully convert from debt to assets that appear on the balance sheet.

Thus, any market in Intellectual Capital would be to support speculation on the potential value of those investments when they become assets and upon the likelihood of their achieving that full value.

Where have we seen that combination of variables before? The i C equation, where C is that potential maximum value and i the chance of the company getting there.

So now we have some interesting tools with which to work. First, we have a two-variable equation by which an organization announces its potential value and its chances of achieving it. We also have a body of metrics about the company, some incorporated in this equation, but many more that are not. The astute speculator could thus obtain a futures contract on this organization's IC—betting, based on his or her own assessment of those IC indices and other factors (such as the departure of a key executive), that this value will change before the Intellectual Capital converts to financial capital.

This would suggest a new sort of futures market for capital stock, using IC measurement tools to evaluate changing market value and underscore contract bidding. This would be consistent with our notion of Intellectual Capital itself: Just as IC reporting is not a replacement to financial accounting, but a prelude to it designed to capture and control some of its more subjective and dynamic components, so, too, the IC exchange would not replace the current capital stock markets but serve as their front-end component, managing their more volatile and unfair (to private investors) elements, and thus restoring to them a measure of order and equality.

What would be the vehicle of this speculation and trade in the IC exchange? It would appear to be a new type of value instrument to replace, or at least enhance, the traditional salary and reward market. The above scenario suggests some form of futures contracts on common stock when the organization is a commercial company, and some sort of nonconvertible futures contract when the organization is not.

Nonprofit and noncommercial organizations first. Obviously these pose some problems. One possibility is that, in some cases, such contracts might indeed be convertible to something like service or tax-deductible donations. In other cases, we have no immediate answer other than that few speculators ever hold commodities contracts at maturity, and that if this noncollateralized nature of speculating in nonprofits proves too high a risk, the exchange can survive without these types of organizations.

Now, for-profit enterprises. Where have we seen this type of speculative, common stock–based instrument before? Of course, our old friend, *employee stock options*. FASB had good reason to worry about them.

One rule we've discovered in studying Intellectual Capital is that, if you follow progressive companies and analysts, they will almost always show you where to look for nascent IC development. Thus, the difference between market capitalization and book value showed us where to find Intellectual Capital. Then the back pages of the annual report scrutinized by smart investors gave us the shape of this new kind of capital. Now, look at a place like Silicon Valley, where employee stock participation hovers near 100 percent, where smart professionals are anxious to trade salary for stock options, and where lending institutions are willing to take these options as collateral for the purchase of cars, homes, and even airplanes. There we can see the kind of exchange we're looking for already in the making.

Of course, there is one little problem: A futures market in common stock would be indistinguishable from speculating on employee stock options—something upon which the SEC in the United States, as well as its counterparts around the world, don't look kindly. Predicting regulatory changes is a game for those who like to be disappointed; nevertheless, it does seem that it would be hard for regulatory agencies to maintain their current stance in the face of a strong and widespread interest to conduct such trade.

An IC-based futures market in common stock is a stunning notion. But now add another wrinkle, once again courtesy of Skandia. In mid-1996, the company initiated the tentative creation of *IC options,* to be used as employee incentives. Such options essentially could be cashed by the employee awardees for a value based upon Skandia's Intellectual Capital performance. Suddenly, instead of a play off existing shares of stock, we have an entirely new speculative instrument specifically linked to IC performance. In this world, the company's two-variable IC valuation would also be the basis for the value of its IC options.

Needless to say, this opens a whole new world of possibilities. Were a sufficient number of companies to offer their employees and investors a significant number of these IC options, an exchange of just these shares would be possible, either alongside or instead of the futures on common shares. This may in fact be the solution to the current regulatory obstacles.

Like other exchanges, an IC exchange would foster the creation of brokerage houses, analysts, conceivably even mutual funds. It surely would also be virtual, probably Internet based, with the buying and selling of shares or contracts and the exchange of information, gossip, and theories racing among millions of sites and involving tens, even hundreds, of millions of private investors.

In fact, the more you ponder it, such an exchange, like many innovations in this virtual age, would incorporate many of the best features of its historic predecessors. Like the New York, London, and Tokyo stock exchanges, it would deal with the creation of organizational value, like the Chicago Mercantile Exchange its mechanism would be futures contracts, and like NASDAQ it would be a free-floating exchange arising from the daily on-line transaction of its multitudes of users. But, in its personality, its intimacy, and its orientation toward human actions and decisions, it would also hark back to Change Alley, standing around Lloyd's coffeeshop swapping gossip and waiting for the next runner to race in with the latest news from the wharf.

PREPARING THE FUTURE

We began this book with a failure and end it with an opportunity. The failure was that of the current financial accounting system to capture the true value of the modern enterprise—and the resulting inequity faced by small individual investors when competing with professional investors. Our goal was to identify those intangible factors off the balance sheet, measure them, and find a way to present them in a coherent way.

The result was a model for visualizing and reporting Intellectual Capital. It centered around a navigational tool that acted as an organizer for the different types of value-laden corporate investments, and that offered a more balanced and holistic perspective than traditional models.

That, in turn, led us to establish a body of measurements that best captured the essence of each of these types. What we discovered were two important facts. The first was that these measurements came in three forms, and that two of these could be reduced to a pair of variables that would act as a simple measure of IC performance that could be compared with the same measure for other firms. The second was that, being detached from traditional revenues and profit and loss statements, this measure would also apply to other noncommercial organizations, including government and nonprofit institutions—making such a comparison possible for the first time.

The existence of this new value measurement system, as well as the IC common measure, opens the possibility of making a market in the speculation of Intellectual Capital and thus creating a brand-new reward system. The instrument of this market might be futures contracts on capital stock, or in the latest innovation, newly minted IC stock options.

And with that we come nearly full circle. What started as a search for true value and fairness to investors ends with an important new opportunity for those investors. Does that start the circle again as the advantages in this new market grow unequal? Perhaps in time, as we enter the next technological revolution. But for now, the measurement of Intellectual Capital brings accounting and investing back into alignment with the radical changes that are taking place in the corporation. And in its breadth it also captures the erasure of boundaries between companies and other institutions that is right now occurring everywhere in our society.

And after all, isn't this congruence, this reflection of the way we live today, the underlying value of all financial accounting?

Rather than replacing the current financial measurement system, the product of generations, Intellectual Capital measurement in fact complements and augments it. Orthodox accounting has found its way again. It is relevant once more to our future. And thus the work of much of the last millennium is made ready for the next.

Notes

CHAPTER 1

1. "Rest in Peace, Book Value," *Forbes ASAP,* October 25, 1993, p. 9.
2. Walter Wriston, "The Twilight of Sovereignty" (New York: Scribner's, 1992).
3. From an interview with Steven M.H. Wallman. The quote appeared in an article by Michael S. Malone in the *Los Angeles Times,* 1995.
4. Ibid.
5. Ibid.
6. Polly LaBarre, "The Rush on Knowledge," *Industry Week,* February 19, 1996, p. 53.
7. Ibid., pp. 53–54.
8. Author interview with Prof. Hamel, July 1996.
9. Ibid.
10. Source: Prof. Baruch Lev, UC Berkeley and Stern School of Business, New York University.
11. Keith Bradley. "Intellectual Capital and the New Wealth of Nations." Lecture given at the Royal Society of Arts, London, October 21, 1996; p. 6 in author's document. Bracketed section from footnote to passage in document.
12. Tom Stewart, "Your Company's Most Valuable Asset: Intellectual Capital," *Fortune,* October 3, 1994, cover story.
13. Sarah Mavrinac and Terry Boyle, "Sell-Side Analysis, Non-Financial Performance Evaluation and the Accuracy of Short-Term Earnings Forecasts," an Ernst & Young Boston Center for Information Technology and Strategy working paper, September 1996, p. 2.

14. Ibid., p. 1. Emphasis added.
15. Ibid.
16. Ibid.
17. Ibid.
18. *Lifting All Boats: Increasing the Payoff from Private Investment in the U.S. Economy,* Competitiveness Policy Council report, September 1995.
19. Karl-Eric Sveiby, *Knowledge Focused Strategy: How to Manage and Measure Intangible Assets,* in manuscript, dated August 6, 1996; forthcoming book 1997.
20. See: Bo Hedberg, *Imaginary Organizations,* Liber-Hermods, Stockholm, 1996.
21. This difference was noticed decades ago by James Tobin as well as John Kenneth Galbraith. Tobin's research led to the so-called Tobin's variable "q," which equals market value/book value.
22. Ibid.
23. Ibid.
24. Ibid.
25. Ibid.
26. Leif Edvinsson, *Intellectual Capital, A Strategic Inquiry by Paradigm Pioneers,* booklet, 1994.
27. "The Coins in the Knowledge Bank," *Fortune,* February 19, 1996. Taken off the Internet.
28. *Visualizing Intellectual Capital in Skandia,* Supplement to Skandia's 1994 Annual Report, p. 6.
29. Ibid., pp. 6–7.
30. Charles Savage, *Fifth Generation Management* (USA: Butterworth-Heinemann) 1996.
31. Mr. Armstrong is CEO of Armstrong World Industries.
32. Karl-Eric Sveiby, "Towards a Framework for Our IC Dialogue," *The Knowledge Organization* (London: Barret-Koehler).

CHAPTER 2

1. Peter J. Eisen, *Accounting* (Hauppauge, NY: Barron's Educational Series), p. 264.
2. *Only the Paranoid Survive* (New York: Currency Books/Doubleday), pp. 141–42.

3. Based on comments by Leif Edvinsson, published in "Skandia Assurance and Financial Services (A): Measuring Intellectual Capital" by David Oliver, International Institute for Management Development (Switzerland) report, June 12, 1995.

4. One interesting quick measure of a company's Human Capital is to take the discounted net present value of average earnings per employee over average employment time.

5. "The Rush on Knowledge," p. 56.

6. See the Skandia value scheme, chapter 3.

7. The model was originally created by the Skandia team.

8. Cian Molloy, "From IQ to Ecu," *Human Resources Banking and Insurance* (London: Lafferty Publications) February 1995, pp. 8–9.

9. Knowledge organization expert Karl Sveiby divides these three classifications as "Employees' Competence," "Internal Structure," and "External Structure." See *Knowledge Focused Strategy: How to Manage and Measure Intangible Assets.*

10. A quick measure of customer capital: discounted net present value of average earnings per customer relationship over the length of the relationship.

11. "From IQ to Ecu," p. 8.

12. Ibid.

13. Yet another etymological note: In English, the term "capital" applies not only to measurements of wealth, but also, in keeping with its Latin roots, to "head" or "large," as in capital letters and a capital city. Implicit in this is the notion that financial capital is a centralized, monolithic activity—just the opposite of where capital usually resides in the modern organization.

14. "From IQ to Ecu," p. 8.

15. Ibid., p. 9.

16. *Knowledge Focused Strategy: How to Manage and Measure Intangible Assets,* p. 47.

CHAPTER 3

1. "How to Value Service Organizations," (Stockholm: The Swedish Coalition of Service Industries) 1992.

2. For the record, the Skandia IC team members at the time of the first public IC annual report included among others, Tove Husell, Marie Kjellvertz, Peter Westoo, Barbro Ericsson, Mikael Selin, Joacim Lindgren, and Ingela Lispers, as well as Leif Edvinsson.
3. Credit for these building blocks belongs to senior vice president Lars Lekander, now retired Skandia AFS growth strategist.
4. L. Edvinsson and P. Sullivan, "Intellectual Capital Management," *European Management Journal,* Dec. 1996.

CHAPTER 4

1. "The Rush on Knowledge," p. 54.
2. *Knowledge Focused Strategy How to Manage and Measure Intangible Assets,* p. 48.
3. See: James Brian Quinn, *The Intelligent Enterprise.*
4. One such effort, called Evita, is under development by ABB.
5. Baruch Lev: Boundaries on Financial Reporting, SEC Symposium, April 1996.

CHAPTER 5

1. Johan Roos and Göran Roos, *IC Visualizing and Measuring,* in manuscript; forthcoming book from (London: Macmillan Business) 1997.
2. This is comparable to leveraging off the company's second life cycle curve. See *The Second Curve: Managing the Velocity of Change* by Ian Morrison (New York: Ballantine Books, 1996).

CHAPTER 6

1. Debra M. Amadon, *Knowledge Innovation Strategy*, in manuscript.
2. Don Tapscott, *The Digital Economy* (New York: McGraw-Hill, 1996).

3. William Davidow and Michael S. Malone, *The Virtual Corporation* (New York: HarperCollins, 1994).

CHAPTER 7

1. R. Kaplan and D. Norton, *The Balanced Scorecard* (Boston: HBS Press, 1996).
2. Tom Davenport, *Process Innovation* (Boston: HBS Press, 1993).

CHAPTER 8

1. What is missing from IC measurement that also contributes to a company's character and resilience is a strong company history, myth, and philosophy of doing business. See *Built to Last: Successful Habits of Visionary Companies,* by James C. Collins and Jerry I. Porras (New York: HarperBusiness, 1994).

CHAPTER 9

1. Riel Miller and Gregory Wurzburg, "Investing in Human Capital," *The OECD Observer,* April–May 1995, p. 16.
2. Ibid., p. 17.
3. Ibid.
4. Ibid., pp. 17–18.
5. Ibid., p. 18.

CHAPTER 10

1. Source for this section is *Knowledge Focused Strategy: How to Manage and Measure Intangible Assets.*
2. Annie Brooking, *Intellectual Capital: Core Asset for the Third Millennium Enterprise* (London: International Thomson Business

Press, 1996). This book is good for company executives developing an internal company rationale for instituting an IC measurement program.

3. Ibid., p. 83.
4. Ibid., pp. 83–85.
5. Ibid., p. 84.
6. Ibid., p. 85.
7. From a private conversation, San Jose, California,

CHAPTER 11

1. G. Pascal Zachary, "High Tech Is Forming a Role as an Indicator," *The Wall Street Journal,* September 30, 1996, p. 1A.
2. The following historical material is derived from Michael S. Malone, "Is Silicon Valley over the Hill?" *Upside,* April 1994, pp. 12–13.

CHAPTER 12

1. Steven Albert and Keith Bradley, "The Management of Intellectual Capital," report of Business Performance Group Ltd. (London School of Economics), February 1995, p. 102.
2. Ferdinand Braudel, *Civilization and Capitalism, 15th–18th Century, The Wheels of Commerce* (London: William Collins, 1985).
3. "The Management of Intellectual Capital," Chapter 12: Knowledge Exchanges, pp. 101–107.
4. Ibid., p. 102.
5. Ibid.
6. Ibid., p. 104.
7. Ibid.
8. See Bradley's "The New Wealth of Nations" for his latest thoughts on the subject.

Index